Love
and Ideology
in the Afternoon

Arts and Politics of the Everyday
Patricia Mellencamp, Meaghan Morris, Andrew Ross, series editors

Love
and Ideology
in the Afternoon
Soap Opera,
Women, and
Television Genre

■

Laura Stempel Mumford

INDIANA UNIVERSITY PRESS
BLOOMINGTON & INDIANAPOLIS

The paper used in this publication meets the minimum requirements of American National Standard for Information Sciences—Permanence of Paper for Printed Library Materials, ANSI Z39.48-1984. ∞™

Manufactured in the United States of America

Library of Congress Cataloging-in-Publication Data

Mumford, Laura Stempel.
   Love and ideology in the afternoon: soap opera, women, and television genre / Laura Stempel Mumford.
      p.   cm. — (Arts and politics of the everyday)
   Includes bibliographical references and index.
   ISBN 0-253-32879-9 (cl). — ISBN 0-253-20965-X (pb)
   1. Soap operas—United States—Criticism and interpretation. 2. Television and women—United States. 3. Television viewers—United States. I. Title. II. Series.
PN1992.8.S4M86   1995
791.45'6—dc20   94-44239

1   2   3   4   5   00   99   98   97   96   95

Contents

■

ACKNOWLEDGMENTS

■ The acknowledgments page, with its long list of friends, colleagues, and institutions "whose support and encouragement made this project possible," has become an obligatory academic ritual, but for those of us who work on the margins of the formal academy, it is, I think, one of the most meaningful and important gestures we can make. For so-called "independent scholars," the struggle to construct a community within which to work can be far more difficult than the most intimidating confrontation with the blank page, and this is sometimes the only opportunity we have to thank the people who have helped us continue to imagine ourselves as scholars. It is impossible for me to convey how deeply I appreciate those who have so generously volunteered to be my colleagues over the years, and their support is all the more precious because no institutional structure required it of them.

Thanks to Pat Mellencamp and Charlotte Brunsdon for their enthusiasm about this book, and for their extremely valuable advice about the final version; to Ellen Berry, JoAnn Castagna, Barb Klinger, and Lynn Spigel for their helpful contributions to earlier versions of chapter 5; to Tania Modleski for her suggestions about an earlier version of chapter 4; and to Harriet Margolis for taking the time to read and comment so carefully on large parts of the manuscript. To my annual MMLA Women's Caucus dinner companions, especially Frances Kavenik and Carol Klimick Cyganowski, my profound appreciation for years of professional support and rowdy meals. I'm also indebted to all of the people with whom I've watched and talked about the soaps—including my mother, Roslyn K. Stempel, who hates the genre but asks good questions, some of which led me to the argument of chapter 3.

Closer to home, I'm immensely grateful to Dean Robbins for seeing what I could do as a writer and giving me what was for more than eight years the perfect venue in which to do it; to Julie D'Acci for many happy hours of goal setting and just the push I needed to finish this book; to Diane Worzala for a life-saving lunch tradition; and to Bob Buchanan, Judy Davidoff, Cathy Harding, Chip Quadde, and Jan Stempel for various kinds of fun and attention.

Finally, several people have not only made my work as a scholar and writer possible through their contributions to this and other projects, but have made my daily life happy in ways I can only begin to enumerate. I owe more than I can fit on this page to Betsy Draine for her friendship, collegiality, and sympathy; to Kent Williams for all of those things, plus his kind last-minute reading; and to Gary Sosnick, who got me into this in the first place, for being at the other end of the phone line.

And thanks most of all to Bob, who takes me seriously and laughs in all the right places.

Earlier versions of chapter 5 appeared in *Genders* 12 (Winter 1991): 45–61, and in *To Be Continued . . . Soap Operas around the World,* ed. Robert C. Allen (London: Routledge, 1994), pp. 164–81. An earlier version of chapter 4 appeared in *Quarterly Review of Film and Video* 15, no. 2 (1993): 57–74.

*Love
and Ideology
in the Afternoon*

1

Viewing Histories and Textual Difficulties

Perhaps the most common type of difficulty in U.S. . . . television series is *prior narrative dependence*. . . . Soap operas epitomize this practice. . . .

—Brad Chisholm, "Difficult Viewing"

When we speak our selves within theoretical contexts . . . the coherency of the self is opened up and its movement into theory creates the possibility of other positions.

—Elspeth Probyn, *Sexing the Self*

■ I began watching soap operas in 1969. I was about 17, and like many viewers, I was introduced to the programs by an initiate. In my case, however, it wasn't the mother or grandmother who crops up in so many ethnographies, for none of the upper-middle-class, liberal, vaguely intellectual women and girls around whom I grew up watched—or would admit to watching—soaps. Instead, it was my high school boyfriend who introduced me to the pleasures of the soap opera text. Long before high-profile storylines like Luke and Laura's *General Hospital* wedding pumped up the male audience for daytime soaps, and even before *All My Children* targeted teenagers, we would lounge around his house after school, watching the black-and-white half-hours of angst and intrigue. If we identified with the characters, or even talked about the storylines, I don't remember it now. But I do remember that soaps seemed for the first time, not some debased form that could only interest bored and not very bright housewives with nothing better to do, but a part of the popular culture in which we immersed ourselves every day, connected to the music we listened to and the prime-time shows we watched. Although I couldn't have expressed it in these terms at the time, I recognized the value judgments and class prejudices implicit in the prevailing distaste for soap opera and those who watched it, and my soap habit arose at least in part from a desire to embrace a genre I knew my parents and other high-culture affiliates detested.

In college, I watched more sporadically, gathering some of the women in my dorm to watch the *Dark Shadows* finale on a borrowed TV, catching occasional episodes of *General Hospital* or *Days of Our Lives*—just enough to keep track of the characters, but without much investment in the stories themselves. Ironically, it wasn't until I got to graduate school in the mid-1970s and joined a self-consciously intellectual community that I suddenly found a cohort of women, and one or two men, who also watched soaps. As feminists, we had a special interest in and attachment to the cultural forms traditionally consumed by women, and all around us, intellectuals were coming out as lovers of popular culture. But watching soap operas was no mere political or theoretical gesture. Instead, it was a gesture toward fun, a commitment undertaken for the pleasure of the narrative itself, the comfort of habitual viewing, and the communal enjoyment of talking about the programs.

It was inevitable that, as I became a more sophisticated and professionalized student of culture, my experience of the soaps would be influenced by the literary and feminist theory I was learning. Although I had always been a critical spectator, prone to screaming at the TV set, my tendency to question what I watched increased as I acquired specific analytical tools and a vocabulary in which to frame my opinions, yet I continued to be drawn to the shows primarily because of my curiosity about the stories. Eventually, I found myself stranded without the serious prospect of a teaching career, forced to reconsider some of my scholarly commitments, certain that I wanted to keep writing, and drawn slowly by my interest in soap opera away from turn-of-the-century feminist theory and novels and into television studies. I began to retrain myself in the field, to try to organize some of my ideas about soaps into conference presentations and articles, and when I left the formal academy for good and began to write a newspaper column about television, my very first subject was the soaps. But once again, this was not merely a professional choice: I wrote about soaps, then as now, because I watched them, because I was interested in thinking about how they work, and because I wondered why I enjoy them so much.

I begin with this history, not simply to prove my credentials as a "real" soap opera viewer, or to demonstrate the expertise with which I can unravel certain programs' "prior narrative dependence,"[1] but to illustrate how my own involvement with soaps has both shifted and remained stable over time. The central attraction has always been narrative—what will happen next?—yet that simple magnetism has rarely been my only interest. My intellectual interests and social allegiances have shaped both my viewing habits and my attitude toward and understanding of the programs themselves: I began watching, after all, in order to spend time with my boyfriend, to enjoy what he was enjoying, and if my loyalty to the genre has outlasted his own interest in soaps by nearly 25 years, I owe to him the fact that I'm watching *General Hospital* today. For nearly a decade, I kept up with the programs we watched together, reevaluating them for the first time only in the late 1970s, when the shift from a 30- to a 60-minute format made it impossible, in that pre-VCR age, to watch so many different serials in a day.

I could tell a similar story about each soap opera I watch: how I became interested in one show because it was a favorite of some of the women with whom I shared my soap enthusiasm, or stuck with another during slow periods because it was the only one other friends watched; how I came back to a series I'd dropped in order to follow an unusual storyline, or switched to another to get a better sampling of the genre. So, too, my viewing habits have oscillated as my interests and work routines changed. There have been years in which I barely missed an episode of a favorite show and others in which I barely caught one; months when, thanks to my VCR, I watched five or six programs a day, and months when I listened to the radio instead. More often, though, I've watched a regular set of shows several times a week, usually in the distracted fashion for which soap opera viewers are famous: I wrote my dissertation while watching the soaps, and I'm still usually reading or writing at the same time. (There's been plenty of theorizing about how the complexly redundant narrative structure of soaps enables women to watch while performing domestic chores. Perhaps it's time to give some thought to that structure's intersection with the rhythms of writing!)

There are, of course, certain potential dangers in making my own experience the touchstone of a theory about how soap operas work, but those dangers are not, I think, inevitable. As Elspeth Probyn argues,

> the centrality of the critic's experience [does not] necessarily reify her as the organizing principle of critical discourse. It merely serves to alert the critic that there is always something else going on. . . . [Nor is it] some sort of guarantee of the authenticity either of the text or of the critic's reading. Rather, it directs us to look at the ways in which the critic's experience of what he or she describes is a crucial part of an overall critical intervention.[2]

By locating the following argument within my own history as a soap opera viewer, I hope to avoid from the outset the us/them dichotomy that has plagued many analyses of the genre. Although much recent feminist and cultural studies–influenced work has attempted to avoid this pitfall, earlier studies often rested on the assumption, not always made explicit, that the critic/theorist is not part of the audience she describes.[3] As a longtime soap watcher who is also a critic and theorist, I cannot easily separate myself from the rest of the soap opera audience, cannot define that audience as a "them" from whom I sit apart, cannot insist that I am baffled by "their" enjoyment of a form that is transparently commercial, sexist, or petty. The question "why do *I* like these shows?" lies at the root of this book, which represents not simply a theoretical intervention in the field, but my own struggle to reconcile my pleasure in the genre with my recognition of the form's tendencies to reproduce the repressive ideology of capitalist patriarchy.

Neither can I lay claim, however, to some kind of spectatorial innocence that gives me direct access to the reception practices of viewers who are not professional critics. Even if I believed that such transparency were possible, and that it could in turn be transcribed in a format like this one, it would be as foolish for me to claim that my critical and theoretical privilege makes no difference at all in how I watch as to contend that I am never swept up by the pleasures of the programs' narrative. I bring to my experience of soaps a set of tools and a degree of self-consciousness about my own viewing processes that not everyone possesses. I am a fan, but not merely a fan; a critic, but never simply a critic.

Because so much of the soap opera audience has, as I do, a long history with the genre and with particular programs, it is crucial to distinguish the specific expertise that arises from such a history from the more generalized competence—what Charlotte Brunsdon calls "the culturally constructed skills of femininity"[4]—that might be needed to make sense of the genre in the first place. For that reason I want to begin by outlining a typology of soap opera viewing competence, ranging from the inexperienced or *incompetent* viewer—one who has never watched a soap—to the *expert*, who has a long history with the genre as a whole and with one or more individual shows. The incompetent viewer, who knows nothing of soap opera convention or history, will understand little of an episode, and because of its self-referential, nonlinear structure, may not even be able to make sense of it in the most superficial way. An expert, on the other hand, will bring a wealth of historical memory and detailed information to the viewing experience, and therefore will, if she watches attentively, understand nearly everything she sees: the characters, their motivations, the relationships among them, and thus the background and potential consequences of particular narrative developments.[5]

In between those two poles I would place, in order of increasing expertise, the *novice*, also a newcomer to the genre, but one whose interest in learning its rules marks her difference from the incompetent viewer; the *casual* viewer, with some experience of the form, but no particular history with or commitment to any specific show; the *irregular* viewer, who may have a long history but watches infrequently, or whose habitual viewing may be interrupted for long periods of time (by, say, a change in work or domestic routine); and the *competent* viewer, who has regular viewing habits and some history, but lacks the detailed historical memory conferred by years of experience.

These are, of course, highly subjective, relative, and in some sense even arbitrary terms, for a person who considers herself an expert after, say, two or three years of watching a soap may find herself feeling merely competent alongside someone with a 10- or 20-year viewing history. It is also important to note that a single viewer can belong to more than one of these categories, depending on whether we are talking about expertise in the genre or in a particular program. For instance, because of my long history of watching soap operas, I would consider myself expert not only in the genre, but in several individual programs—*General Hospital, All My Children, The Young and the Restless*—as well. Yet my shorter viewing history with *Another World* makes me only competent about its characters' complex genealogies and densely entangled pasts. (In fact, an unanticipated benefit of my adoption of this program was a reminder of the apprenticeship required before a new viewer becomes truly competent.) Similarly, although I have a certain amount of expertise based on many years of watching *One Life to Live* or *Days of Our Lives*, the fact that I now see them only occasionally means that I am currently a competent viewer at best: I know the shows' distant past far more intimately than their recent history, yet that knowledge allows me to understand at least some of what I see, even if months have passed since I last saw an episode. The fact that I watch other current soaps a few times a year clearly makes me an irregular viewer of some of them, and merely casual toward others.

Yet as an expert consumer of the genre, I can never be a true novice when I watch a new show, because my knowledge of the conventions, story formulas, and narrative rules gives me an immediate way of understanding even a program whose characters and history are unfamiliar to me. My inability to recapture that original naive viewing position rests, I should emphasize, on my own history with the genre—shared by all expert and competent soap opera viewers—rather than on my expertise as a scholar of the form. We might, in fact, argue that soap operas' generic rules circulate so broadly via prime-time serials, parodies, feature films, commercial allusions, and other references that few viewers with any experience of mainstream popular culture can now be truly incompetent in the form. (Still, even though we may have some difficulty finding many real viewers who are so unfamiliar with soap opera as to be completely incompetent, a scale of expertise requires that we theorize the possibility of such a position.)

This typology of viewer competence underlies my entire analysis of how we watch soap operas, a process that I will argue involves a constant tension between expertise and hope, between anticipation of what we know the genre's formulas and conventions are likely to produce and fantasies about what might change. Clearly, such a typology is connected to the idea that soaps, like other cultural forms, offer a set of preferred readings to an imagined set of ideal readers.[6] Although readers—or in this case, viewers—are to some extent free to reject or resist the dominant meaning of the soap opera text, they must begin with that text's attempts to position them and, in the case of mainstream commercial media artifacts like soap operas, that positioning is emphasized by the heavy weight of dominant ideology. "Resistant" and "oppositional" readings, those that go "against the grain," by definition do so by refusing or running counter to those readings offered by the text's producers and reinforced by the surrounding culture. (In Stuart Hall's words, the "oppositional" viewer "detotalizes the message in the preferred code in order to retotalize the message within some alternative framework of reference.")[7] I would argue that soap opera's ideal readers—the viewers imagined by the text's producers and positioned to understand most of its details—belong to the groups I have identified as "competent" and "expert." Soaps provide many aids that permit relatively inexperienced viewers to make sense of their narratives, including backstory, repetition, dialogue whose sole purpose is exposition, extremely slow story development, and the use of conventions drawn from other familiar dramatic forms; but competent and expert viewers are able to understand the most—and therefore, not coincidentally, to receive the greatest pleasure from the form.

In a sense, these viewers—or better, their competence as viewers—are a creation of the text itself, for it is through watching soaps that we gain the experience necessary to decode further episodes and new series. A soap opera teaches us how to watch it, tutors us in its rules and conventions, provides us with the history and information we need, and thus makes it possible for us to understand it in the future. I do not mean to suggest in any way, however, that soap viewers—or consumers of any other cultural artifacts—are passive recipients of producers' all-powerful texts, much less that we are simply discursive constructs created by the programs we watch. Indeed, I want to acknowledge from the outset not only television viewers' existence beyond the discourse of television, but our work as collaborators in the construction of the soap opera (and every other) text. The very notion of viewer competence, at least as I am invoking it, assumes that there is active work to be done in watching soaps, especially in sorting through our knowledge of the genre's rules and our memories of a program's short- and long-term history as we attempt to make sense of each new event on the screen.

Nevertheless, throughout this book my argument emphasizes viewers' role as recipients, albeit active ones, of a text produced elsewhere, by writers, producers, and actors, technical workers, production companies, and the commercial television networks by and for whom the programs are made. In this context, Charlotte Brunsdon's insistence that, "difficult as it may be, we have to retain a notion of the television text" is especially important for me.[8] I presume that there is a text which in some sense preexists viewers' consumption of it, and which continues to exist to a great extent beyond viewers' reach, a situation that is illuminated by Brad Chisholm's distinction between television and chess: "We might differentiate the 'active' playing of chess from the 'reactive' viewing of television by the criterion of being able to influence the outcome. We affect the direction of a chess game with every move, but no matter how hard we hypothesize as we untangle a [storyline], we cannot affect the outcome of a screen narrative."[9]

A focus on the text need not preclude a concern with the mechanisms by which it is consumed, for, as Christine Gledhill suggests, "the textual critic analyses the *conditions and possibilities of reading.*"[10] But despite the often compelling claims of audience research and my own interest in thinking about how people, and women in particular, watch soaps, I believe that before we can consider what viewers do with a television text, we must make an effort to describe that text. My analysis is thus first of all a consideration of how the *narratives* of soap operas work, rather than one that focuses primarily on how we watch them.

Instead of outlining in advance of my argument the rest of the rather eclectic theoretical apparatus that underpins this book, I prefer to introduce the individual parts of that apparatus as the specific issues arise, but I do want to offer one or two important caveats before I begin. While I will make references throughout my analysis to the differences and occasional similarities between "real life" and the fictional world of soap operas, I do not intend either to claim an inevitable opposition between them or to read any television program or genre as an unmediated mirror image of some objective "reality." Despite the complexity with which television imitates, distorts, and recuperates viewers' conceptions of reality, it seems apparent to me that any ideological analysis—and this is certainly one—necessarily rests on the notion that there is some tie between the two.[11] I assume, for instance, that while they are clearly artificial constructions, and are understood as such by their viewers, soap operas and other apparently realistic fictional programs do present a version of life that viewers can recognize as somehow coherent with their own experience. (Soap operas are in this way distinct from fantasy and science-fiction programs, although some soaps, such as ABC's *One Life to Live* and *General Hospital*, incorporate aspects of those genres. They are also distinct from so-called "reality" and nonfiction programming—*Cops* or *60 Minutes*—that claim to offer less mediated versions of the world around us.) As viewers, we therefore make constant, albeit not always direct or conscious, comparisons between the fictional world of the soaps we watch and the nonfictional world in which we live. This means in turn that we both understand and evaluate the sexual politics and other ideological aspects of the soap opera narrative in terms of the "real" world and come to understand the "real" world to some extent in terms of the programs we watch.

In choosing to analyze soap opera, and to do so from a feminist perspective, I find myself intervening in a number of current debates about popular culture, television, and ideology, as my brief outline of the relationship between television and "reality" makes clear. When we begin to consider the ways in which a popular culture form like the soap opera may or may not work to reinforce the dominant ideology, we immediately recognize just how many apparently basic theoretical issues have yet to be resolved in the field of cultural studies. Even setting aside for the moment questions about what exactly constitutes "the" dominant ideology, the general methods of its enforcement, and the extent to which resistance is possible, there are still major unanswered questions about precisely what television's role could be. In particular, the exact mechanisms by which a TV serial aimed at women might participate in regulating ideology have yet to be delineated to anyone's satisfaction. This is hardly surprising, since arguments persist about whether film—and, if only by implication, television—even constructs any possible viewing position for women.[12]

As feminist critics' recent work on traditional "women's" texts such as soap operas, film melodramas, and romance novels testifies, we can move closer to an understanding of those issues by exploring specific aspects of specific popular texts. Yet this is not to say that there is some simple political or ideological template we can use to evaluate these complicated cultural artifacts. Instead, one of my projects in this book is to demonstrate just how misleading the familiar and seemingly obvious links between, say, a particular narrative strategy and a particular ideological position can actually be.

Still, I do understand the conventional daytime soap opera as having an implicit and at times explicit political agenda, one that I believe cooperates in the "teaching" of male dominance—at the very least, by persuasively restating it, and the related oppressions of racism, classism, and heterosexism, in such a way as to make them seem inevitable, if not necessarily "natural." To avoid a constant reiteration of this chain of "isms," I have chosen to use two specific terms as condensations of the complex power relations that exist throughout the cultures in which soap operas are produced and consumed, and which are at once expressed, perpetuated, contested, and resisted as we watch or think about such programs. The first, *dominant ideology*, refers to the various tightly intertwined economic, social, political, religious, cultural, and other systems and practices that define, express, and maintain the existing power structure. Such power can always be questioned and struggled against, contested and refused, because the systems that support it are variously contradictory, leaky, and unevenly enforced. Yet these systems are also mutually reinforcing, powerfully institutionalized, and woven into the fabric and experience of everyday life in such complex ways as to exert a kind of centripetal force that makes resistance difficult and overthrow even more so. As citizens of a given culture, we are trained throughout our lives to understand and believe in its ideology, to think it "natural" and open to only the most superficial kinds of alterations, even as we recognize the constructed and artificial character of its social manifestations. Perhaps most seductively, we learn to invest and find pleasure in its maintenance, so that it becomes difficult for us all—including members of nondominant and even oppressed groups—to resist the blandishments of the status quo.[13]

Dominant ideology is necessarily conservative in the broadest sense, in that it strives to maintain itself and the status of those in power. But it is also conservative in a more specific sense, identifying and perpetuating a narrow range of "correct" choices in the political, economic, sexual, familial, and other spheres of life. In the case of the United States and other Western and Western-influenced nations, dominant ideology works primarily (although by no means exclusively) in the interests of white, heterosexual, Christian, middle- and upper-middle-class adult men, and its expressions include, among many other features, the veneration of industrial capitalism, individualism, the traditional nuclear family, heterosexual romance, and white racism.

One of the difficulties in invoking this concept of dominant ideology, however, is the ease with which it can be reduced to the notion of an all-powerful force that exists apart from the sphere of individual activity and whose operation somehow takes place beyond the behavior of real people. I therefore want to emphasize the fact that I am not talking about some kind of overarching, magical, and autonomous agent, but instead about a collection of interlocking ideas and relations expressed and worked out precisely through the social interaction between and among individuals. Dominant ideology is not simply imposed from above, nor does it control us completely; instead, it works in and through us in our daily lives, in discourse and in social practice. The system is redundant: a variety of overlapping institutions and practices repeat the same "lessons," helping to assure their continued power. But we also have the capacity to recognize and critique it, to resist or struggle against it in various ways, including through politicized cultural analyses such as this book. This paradox—that we simultaneously occupy positions as both the objects and the agents of dominant ideology—is at the heart not only of the success with which the status quo is maintained, but of my analysis as well.

Since this book deals primarily with the ways in which a specific cultural artifact—soap opera—serves existing ideas about and relations around gender, it is particularly important to have some way of describing the dominant version of those power relations. There are various possibilities—"sexism," for instance, or the less evaluative "sexual politics"—but few seem adequate to describe the systemic and institutional nature of the power relations that surround our ideas about gender. Although it has a vexed history, and has been justifiably critiqued for the ease with which it can be ahistorically applied, I have therefore chosen the term *patriarchy* as a way of referring to the system of male dominance in its broadest sense. Under this rubric I mean to include all of the social, political, cultural, and other ways in which men and masculinity are positioned as superior to women and femininity, among which are many of the same institutions and practices that serve other aspects of dominant ideology, such as the family, government policies, and so on, as well as specific features whose primary function is the perpetuation of women's secondary status. (For example, prevailing standards of female beauty, such as the idea that younger, thinner women are necessarily more attractive than older, heavier ones, work in tandem with the social and commercial arrangements that enforce such standards, such as the beauty industry, which markets products that assist women in conforming to the cultural ideal, as well as marketing, through a wide range of tactics, the *desire* for such products.)

While my use of "patriarchy" is meant to make clear that male dominance is, if not a universal, at least a prevailing ideological feature throughout the world, that dominance necessarily manifests itself in different ways, depending on its specific historical, social, political, and cultural context.[14] The contemporary U.S. version, for instance—what I have condensed as "capitalist patriarchy"[15]—interacts with and mutually reinforces the political system of representative democracy and the economic system of industrial capitalism and tends to work itself out around issues such as women's role in the electoral system, the nuclear family, and the workplace; poor women's rights to reproductive choice; commercial cultural representations of gender; and so on. Like the rest of dominant ideology, the patriarchal status quo is not simply imposed from above, but perpetuated and policed by a variety of institutions and practices, each of which is enacted through social relations and the real-life behavior of individuals. This book offers an explanation of how specific ideas about gender, sexuality, femininity and masculinity, and social women and men are reproduced through a particular part of the cultural apparatus, in this case the television genre of soap opera. Equally important, it offers an analysis of how that particular expression is made to seem so intensely pleasurable that women viewers, including feminists, keep coming back to watch it again and again.

This understanding of the sexual politics and ideological function of soap opera will recur throughout the book, beginning with my return to the question of the soap opera text as I attempt in the next chapter to define the genre and to lay out some of the broad questions facing critics and theorists. In chapter 3, I discuss the ways in which soaps' elision of the public and private spheres—what I identify as the programs' ruling dynamic—works to construct a particular kind of community, while chapter 4 considers the structural and ideological functions of closure in the programs' narrative and in viewers' expectations about particular storylines. The issue of ideology resurfaces most prominently in chapter 5, where I analyze the paternity mystery, a fictional reiteration of the power of the father that seems to me exemplary both of the form's restatement of patriarchy and of its requirement that viewers perform a delicate negotiation between their knowledge of generic traditions and their hope that a particular storyline will take a new and perhaps radical direction. Finally, in chapter 6, I look at some of the extratextual issues that surround soap opera viewing, including the role of commercially produced fan magazines, and suggest the directions in which both my argument and the ongoing evolution of the soap opera might lead. Along the way, I hope that what is in many ways a close reading of the soap opera text will also answer some larger questions about television and its place in the broad landscape of popular culture.

2

What Is This Thing Called Soap Opera?

> The name given to the new genre is as
> interesting as it is unusual. Isn't it unprec-
> edented for a cultural product to indicate so
> crudely its material origin . . . and its conscrip-
> tion in the battle between different commercial
> brands? At the same time, a whole *household*
> definition of a broadcast literature reveals itself
> plainly, making unambiguously clear a twofold
> function: to promote the sale of household
> products, and to subsume the housewife in her
> role by offering her romantic gratification.
>
> —Michele Mattelart, "From Soap to Serial"

■ Despite the close critical and theoretical attention that
has been paid to soap operas over the last decade, few writers have
offered a very clear definition of the genre. Many have identified
general characteristics, compiling lists that may include everything
from major features of the programs' narrative structure to the work
habits of their female characters.[1] Others have remarked on viewers'
understanding of "the poetic and generic rules that govern soap opera programs."[2] Still others have joined Charlotte Brunsdon in calling soap opera "in some ways the paradigmatic television genre (domestic, continuous, contemporary, episodic, repetitive, fragmented,
and aural)."[3] Yet for the most part, theorists have been content to
employ a commonsense definition of the form, such as Robert Allen's

simple equation of soap operas with "daytime dramatic serials."[4] Among the things that have allowed work on soap opera to proceed without a more detailed basic definition is the fact that, as with many other television forms, industry parameters for the original and still–dominant version, U.S. daytime soap operas, have so closely tallied with viewers' understanding of the genre that the category has appeared already to be defined. Because there is little argument over whether or not, for example, *General Hospital* qualifies as a soap, the need for a more precise definition has not seemed especially urgent.

Yet this apparent clarity disappears the moment we move beyond such an obvious example, and the category of soap opera is no longer as transparent as it may once have seemed. The days when all the U.S. programs that could potentially be identified as soap operas shared a clear set of characteristics—notably, daily daytime broadcast—ended with the 1978 debut of *Dallas*, the first major "prime-time soap." Since then, we have watched a seemingly endless set of variations on the soap opera form. Today, the very same commonsense definition that is on one level so self-evident that even relatively inexperienced viewers can immediately recognize, not only that *General Hospital* is a soap opera, but that *SCTV Network*'s "Days of the Week" is a parody of one, dissolves into incoherence when we ask only slightly more complex questions: Are weekly prime-time serials like *Dallas* and *Dynasty* really soaps? What about the murder-centered *Twin Peaks* or the law drama *L.A. Law*? How is it that programs as diverse as the police series *Hill Street Blues* and the family drama *thirtysomething* can both be called soaps?[5] And where do parodies like *Soap* and *Mary Hartman, Mary Hartman*, or productions from Europe and Latin America, fit in?

Efforts have, of course, been made to differentiate among programs like these. Some critics have drawn a line between television serials and other forms of television melodrama (a category that is, as I will argue below, also far less transparent than its usage often suggests), while others have explicitly separated daytime soap operas from so-called "prime-time soaps." Muriel Cantor and Suzanne Pingree, for instance, discriminate between soap operas and prime-time serials such as *Dallas* in terms of production values and costs, number of episodes produced, and content, and Ien Ang makes a similar case when she insists that "[a]n important formal difference between *Dallas* and the daytime soap opera is the much greater attention to visualization in *Dallas*."[6] Because daytime and prime-time serials share so many features and are so often equated,[7] the distinction between them is perhaps the most crucial one, and Gabriele Kreutzner and Ellen Seiter identify two possible stances: regarding prime-time serials as simply "a modification of the US daytime soap opera," or considering series like *Dynasty* and *Dallas* "as an expression of significant changes within the category of texts geared toward an adult audience."[8] Still, the more basic problem of marking soap operas off from programs that exhibit similar characteristics has not been adequately addressed.

A closer look at one attempt to distinguish among closely related program forms suggests just how difficult this task can be. Christine Geraghty's work on soap opera dates back at least to her contributions to the British Film Institute's important 1981 publication *Coronation Street*. Her 1991 book *Women and Soap Opera* can thus be seen as the culmination of over a decade's analysis of both the British and U.S. versions of the television serial. It also represents an attempt to move beyond a text-based understanding of the genre in favor of one that defines soap opera in terms of how viewers make use of it, and thus reflects a major trend in television studies. In *Women and Soap Opera*, Geraghty, a British scholar, equates U.S. daytime, U.S. prime-time, and British serials, calling all of them "soaps." In explaining the principle that unites this group of programs, she writes that "[s]oap operas . . . can now be defined not purely by daytime scheduling or even by a clear appeal to a female audience but by the presence of stories which engage an audience in such a way that they become the subject for public interest and interrogation."[9] As a defining characteristic, however, this produces a category called "soaps" that potentially encompasses nearly all of television. Although Geraghty has in mind the public fascination with the identity of J.R.'s would-be murderer on *Dallas* and speculation about the fates of characters on British serials like *Coronation Street* and *EastEnders*, it is easy to recall other instances of "public interrogation" inspired by programs that can in no way be defined as soap operas, especially in the United States. Think, for instance, of the 1992 debate about Murphy Brown's sitcom pregnancy or the controversy over PBS's 1991 airing of Marlon Riggs's controversial film *Tongues Untied*, to name just two recent U.S. examples.

The problem here is that Geraghty is, quite understandably, trying to define the genre in mainly functional terms, emphasizing what she calls "the capacity of soaps to engage their audiences in the narrative and their ability to open up for public discussion emotional and domestic issues which are normally deemed to be private."[10] Yet we could argue that this capacity is not actually special to soap operas at all, but is instead a characteristic of television as a simultaneously public and domestic medium. As it has done from its beginnings, television introduces public concerns into the private viewing space of the home through news and public affairs programming, fictional uses of current events (sitcoms or crime dramas that incorporate issues from recent headlines), and the presentation of public performances, sports, and political events for consumption in a domestic setting.[11] At the same time, TV's position as the dominant medium of entertainment and information makes it an obvious and constant topic of both private conversation and public discussion. Geraghty implies that, outside of the programs she refers to as "soaps," such talk about television has traditionally focused on subjects that are neither "emotional" nor "domestic," and that it is only through prime-time serials aimed at women that these topics enter the sphere of public talk about TV. Yet cultural-studies-oriented audience research makes it clear that viewers are capable of raising personal issues in connection with programs that encompass a variety of genres.[12] And even if this were not true, the phenomenon of the daytime talk show—*Donahue*, *The Oprah Winfrey Show*, and the like—has institutionalized the public discussion of intensely "private" issues, such as sexuality, domestic violence, parent-child relationships, and so on.[13]

As Geraghty acknowledges, the important thing "is not so much to give [particular programs] the correct label but to recognise why there is a problem about definition."[14] One of the complicating issues is the tendency for television as a whole to incorporate aspects of the melodramatic mode of address into previously established genres, particularly through the increasing personalization of all television expressions, from comedy to the news, a subject to which I will return later in this chapter. Although this has intensified since prime-time serials such as *Dallas* and *Dynasty* became popular, it is a medium-wide trend—at least in the United States, Canada, Australia, and the United Kingdom—and one that renders essentially pointless any strict identification of the personal with soap opera.

To avoid the kind of confusion that arises from a definition that emphasizes function in this way, we need to develop one that focuses instead on the specific characteristics of the genre itself, a definition that allows us not merely to describe and categorize a wide range of programs, but to imagine other possible permutations. Otherwise, theoretical developments will be limited by the fact that those of us who work in the field can never be sure that we are all talking about the same thing. What, for example, does it mean to speak of closure's function in soap opera (to cite only one major theoretical issue) if the "genre" includes daytime and prime-time serials, episodic series that follow a single plot trajectory, episodic series with multiple storylines, and limited-run prime-time series?

Although several important theoretical questions need to be considered before we can examine the following definition in detail, let me begin by specifying as precisely as I can what I mean by the term "soap opera":

> A soap opera is a continuing fictional dramatic television program, presented in multiple serial installments each week, through a narrative composed of interlocking storylines that focus on the relationships within a specific community of characters.

These are the elements I see as "necessary and sufficient to constitute and delimit [the] genre,"[15] and define the term as I will use it throughout this book. Although the traditional U.S. soap opera serves as my primary model, I have deliberately tried to define the form in such a way as to allow for the possibility of a wide range of permutations beyond those that have actually been produced (such as future soaps from nonbroadcast and noncommercial sources and from other than U.S. producers), without sacrificing the specificity that makes a definition useful. Although these parameters are to a great extent derived from commercially produced U.S. daytime serials, there is no reason to imagine that such programs represent the limits of the genre. (At least one national cable service has already produced a serial that meets my criteria, the Christian Broadcasting Network's *Another Life*, which ran from 1981 to 1984.) In particular, we need not expect future examples to be limited to daytime, and the fact that other programs, especially British and Australian serials, already meet most of my criteria suggests that we have by no means seen all the possible variants on the form.

Before I look at the individual elements of my definition in more detail, however, I want to consider why the issue of definition itself has been problematic and to suggest what the effort to define soap opera as a unique genre implies for work on other television forms. The project of genre definition has at least one obvious function for TV theorists: Because it allows us to distinguish among programs that might otherwise seem quite similar, it permits us to separate the operations of specific *forms* (genres) of programming from the operations both of individual televisual *practices*—which may occur in a variety of genres—and of television as a *medium*. (An example of this would be my attempt, above, to separate the formal operations of soap opera from television's capacity as a medium to introduce domestic issues into the public arena.) In the case of soap operas, the need for this kind of separation becomes more and more urgent as conventions traditionally associated with daytime serials bleed into prime time. At least since the U.S. debut of *Dallas*, and certainly since the 1981 premiere of *Hill Street Blues*, televisual practices such as serial-style episodic nonclosure and complexly overlapping storylines have become more and more common on programs that bear few other obvious affinities with daytime soap operas. (Some people might argue that the 1965 debut of *Peyton Place* actually marked the beginning of soap opera's invasion of prime time, but while popular, that series never had *Dallas*'s impact on television conventions.) Jane Feuer has argued that U.S. television exhibits a "general movement . . . towards the continuing serial form."[16] In fact, it is impossible to isolate a single major generic characteristic of soaps—with the possible exception of multiple weekly installments—that is not now also employed by other types of fictional television programs. If we expand the landscape to include nonfiction forms, such as news programs, talk, or game shows, we cannot even except daily presentation.

Nevertheless, certain problems face those who attempt to define specific television genres, and these are not unique to the field of soap opera. A profound theoretical uncertainty underlies most discussions of television form: the lack of an adequate theory of television genre as a whole. While genre has long been a site of debate within film theory, it has only recently begun to be dealt with seriously in television studies. And not surprisingly, questions about the validity of genre itself have accompanied theorists' first serious efforts to move beyond broad generalizations like "television melodrama."

A major objection to the project of genre definition is that television is resistant *as a medium* to the rigidity that such categorization is thought to require. Television is seen, for example, as both the ultimate representative and the primary purveyor of a postmodern sensibility, the site of a self-reflexive mix of ahistorical pastiche and apolitical parody, filled with programs that refer mainly to other programs, and emblematized by MTV. Its fluid formats, argue postmodern theorists, have borders far too permeable to fix into anything that resembles the genres of the past.[17] Others object on the grounds that television categories are too changeable to anchor anything as stable as genre definition, arguing instead that the medium is characterized by constant movement within which, as John Fiske claims, "Each new show shifts genre boundaries and develops definitions."[18]

Yet claims like these seem to ignore a basic characteristic of television, especially in its commercial broadcast incarnation. Indeed, in John Caughie's words, "Questions of genre . . . seem fundamental to television,"[19] particularly in the United States, where television is uniquely genre-driven—not least because the industry obsession with ratings has led producers, broadcasters, and, more recently, cablecasters on a perpetual quest for the programming formula that will guarantee a large and dependable audience. However malleable TV formats may seem, industry self-promotion and trade publications make it clear that programmers rely heavily on viewers' realization that specific programs belong to specific genres. This has several important consequences: While literary and film theorists can, for instance, usefully distinguish between "genre" fiction or movies and other forms, such a distinction is not very useful for television.[20] Even industry discussions of programming innovations demonstrate the importance of a basic genre stability, and most new shows are designed to be immediately recognizable in terms of familiar existing genres, whether as traditional members or as new variations on them. This process is a self-perpetuating one: Programs that viewers find impossible to understand in familiar genre terms tend to be interpreted as mocking audience expectations—as indeed they are, since audiences have been led to expect that new programs will conform to old patterns.

The most prominent recent example of this phenomenon, and one of the most complex demonstrations of the dominance of genre, is *Twin Peaks.* Its initial popularity can probably be attributed to the combined effects of co-creator David Lynch's cult status and the fact that the program's challenges to television conventions—its overt expressions of sexuality and violence, black comedy, allusions to film culture, and so on—seemed at first to take place within a format that mixed the already popular genres of the prime-time serial and the crime/mystery series. Ultimately, however, *Peaks'* loss of audience and both critics' and viewers' intense alienation from the series can, I think, be traced directly to the fact that the audience found it nearly impossible to continue to understand the show in terms of recognizable genres.[21] (It is interesting to note that the few programs that do resist this kind of categorization—including *Twin Peaks*—tend at some point to be identified as soap operas, as if this serves as a default genre.)

An important factor here is the way in which the basic programming structure of U.S. commercial broadcast television (and its noncommercial and cable imitators) interacts with audience expectations to reinforce familiar genre categories. As Caughie has pointed out, "the schedules of the majority viewing channels . . . [concentrate] particular genres and subgenres within the same time-slot: the competition is directed quite blatantly at the same demographic group or taste constituency, and, characteristically, for the network viewer, the choice is *within* genres and subgenres rather than between them."[22] Nowhere is this more evident than in the case of low-caste genres such as soap operas, children's programs, game shows, and talk shows, which tend to be clustered together in fringe time periods. That is not to say that the individual programs within these clusters are identical. Patricia Mellencamp contends that, "While there is still a programming block of time and general set of conventions which define 'soap opera,' each serial is also marked by differentiation," yet such "differentiation" does not necessarily mean, as Mellencamp concludes, that "genre analyses of TV no longer cohere."[23] For both programmers and viewers, genres are to a great extent defined by their placement on the schedule: To place a series in a particular spot on the schedule grid is implicitly to locate it within a particular genre.

The centrality of genre to the operations of the TV industry, then, makes it ironic that, while specific individual forms such as soap operas and sitcoms have received an enormous amount of analytic attention, television genre theory itself is still at a relatively early stage of development. What Caughie calls "assumptions of genre" pervade TV studies, but major books on television form have only recently begun automatically to include detailed discussions of genre theory, and that theory has only begun to deal with the impact of television's unique combination of repetition and difference on notions of genre.[24]

One reason for this late start is the relatively recent separation of television studies from the study of film and literature. Although the issue of television's difference from film was raised early on, it has taken a long time for critics and theorists to recognize just how limited an application there may be in TV for concepts originally developed for the study of film.[25] Much work continues to draw on film theory, but it is crucial to remember that, in Jane Feuer's words, "television as an apparatus differs in almost every significant respect from cinema."[26] The role of the major U.S. broadcast networks in shaping the television programming agenda, the effect of commercials on the narrative structure of individual programs, the simultaneous availability of anywhere from 4 to 150 viewing options, the networks' changing relationships both to their affiliates and to cable services, and the domestic setting in which television is consumed are only a few of the things that set the medium apart from film.

This insight is particularly important in the case of soap opera, which has almost universally been understood as a form of melodrama, and therefore has frequently been discussed using the analyses developed for the stage and film versions of it. Melodrama may be invoked as a meta-genre, a mode of address, a form of imagination, or a performance style. Or it may be used as a blanket term that means roughly the same thing as "television drama," as David Thorburn seems to do when he includes in the category of TV melodrama "most made-for-television movies, the soap operas, and all the lawyers, cowboys, cops and docs, the fugitives and adventurers, the fraternal and filial comrades who have filled the prime hours of so many American nights for the last thirty years."[27] But paradoxically, as melodrama comes to be—and to be seen as—the dominant mode of television expression, its usefulness as a way of understanding a specific genre such as soap opera becomes more and more limited.

In "Melodrama Inside and Outside the Home," Laura Mulvey traces the development of what she variously calls the "melodramatic style" and the "melodramatic aesthetic" from the eighteenth- and nineteenth-century stage through Hollywood cinema and finally "to its death in the television-dominated home."[28] In its stage incarnation, melodrama is characterized by exaggerated gestures and a plot more dependent on fate than on individual heroic action, while Hollywood film versions focus on women and the home, sexuality, repression, and a conflict between the individual and an intrusive community. Finally, says Mulvey, in television, "[t]he long-standing tension between inside"—home, sexuality, emotion—"and outside is resolved": melodrama, which originally depended on public theatrical expressions of private emotions, becomes totally absorbed into the home when it is consumed via the domesticated medium of television.[29]

Mulvey seems to imply that television melodrama is essentially impossible, its necessarily public character canceled out when it is consumed in the home. But according to Lynne Joyrich, we can instead see melodrama as "the preferred form for TV."[30] Joyrich points out daytime and prime-time serials' employment of specific stylistic markers associated with melodrama, such as "[t]he use of music to convey emotional effects" and the heightening of dramatic moments through "concentrated visual metaphors" (p. 131), but she argues that melodrama "so dominates [television's] discourse that it becomes difficult to locate as a separate TV genre" (p. 131). Although she draws on Thorburn's argument, her claim here is quite different from his sweeping generalizations, resting as it does on an analysis of postmodern consumerism and the ways in which the personal and domestic framework characteristic of film melodrama has come to enclose a wide range of television forms, from made-for-TV movies to police dramas to the stories on the evening news. Still, she admits that, "as it spreads across a number of TV forms . . . melodrama loses its specificity, becoming diffuse and ungrounded in its multiple deployments in the flow of TV" (p. 135).

Joyrich's argument is extremely persuasive, and several of the traits she assigns to melodrama will be important later in this book—among them the externalization of internal conflicts, the perpetuation of the myth of the total legibility of meaning, an intense concern with gender, and the way that framing a story in exclusively personal terms allows the framer to evade its ideological implications. Yet the essay raises a serious problem for work on television genres that have traditionally been considered melodramas, for the increasing diffuseness Joyrich describes applies as much to the usefulness of the *concept* of melodrama as to its presence on the program grid. If melodrama is seen as TV's dominant mode of address, its dominant aesthetic, or the meta-genre that subsumes the majority of television genres—and I think it may be all of these at once—then there is limited value in discussing specific genres such as soap opera primarily in terms of their melodramatic nature. In other words, even if almost all of television is melodramatic, we still need to distinguish soap opera from the other melodramatic genres that fill the airwaves. An understanding of melodrama must certainly inform any serious discussions of soap opera, but we are still left with much the same question we have always needed to ask: how is soap opera different from other television genres?

At the same time, melodrama's very pervasiveness reminds us once again of the necessity of questioning the extent to which we can usefully employ filmic (or theatrical or literary) concepts in discussions of television. In its heyday from the 1930s to the 1950s, after all, film melodrama was only one of a number of different cinematic forms. Although some, such as film noir, were inflected by it, few film genres were actually transformed *into* melodrama, as so much of television has been.[31] At the very least, as Robyn Wiegman insists in her analysis of TV's presentation of the 1991 Gulf War, "melodrama must be understood, in its televisual deployment, as a 'contaminated' genre: cutting, mixing, and otherwise transforming the representational strategies we associate with it from the study of cinema."[32] Television *takes up* melodramatic strategies, as it takes up strategies employed by other film, stage, and literary traditions, such as the domestic novel, the mystery, vaudeville, the film musical, and so on. But rather than simply being transplanted to television, these features are adapted and transformed into specifically televisual strategies; while never wholly severed from other media, they follow a specific developmental trajectory within television.

In fact, there may be good reason to question even a broad equation of soap opera with melodrama. Christine Gledhill has drawn attention to the ambiguous historical and theoretical relationships between the two, tracing the ties between melodrama and a variety of "women's" fictions, including the domestic novel, film melodramas, and both radio and TV soaps.[33] She argues that soap opera's emphasis on dialogue undermines melodrama's dependence on gestural and metaphoric expressions of emotion, while serialization is antagonistic to what she describes as melodrama's "deus-ex-machina resolutions" (p. 113). Although Gledhill acknowledges that the forms share a number of mechanisms—including a heavy reliance on stories involving coincidence, mysteries about parentage, and the reappearance of long-lost characters—she suggests that melodrama and soap opera actually constitute separate narrative strategies for dealing with the realm of the personal. One of her most intriguing insights is that soap opera's much-publicized ability to deal with social issues is the result of a kind of handoff from melodrama to strategies specific to soaps: "once melodrama has put the problem on the agenda, soap opera's diagnostic technique of conversation will frequently dissipate the melodramatic charge as characters chew over . . . the emotional, moral, and social implications and consequences of the event" (p. 121).

Questions of genre necessarily also raise questions about the complex relationship between a medium and its audience and about the site(s) at which meaning is produced. In the case of television studies, the reluctance to dwell on genre definitions is probably connected to the fact that much contemporary criticism and theory developed in reaction both to social-science-based audience studies organized around issues of "influence" and to textual analyses growing out of film and literary studies. The resulting work has emphasized the notion of active viewers who make meaning through their encounters with polysemous television texts, and has shifted attention away from textually based studies. As I suggested in my discussion of Christine Geraghty's functional approach, this acknowledgment of viewers' role in the production of meaning has some clear implications for defining soap opera in particular. Yet, since one of the major projects of genre study is to group individual texts according to their shared formal characteristics, texts must necessarily be the basis of any notion of genre.

This is an especially vexing problem in television studies, for many theorists agree that what Robyn Wiegman calls television's "permeable borders . . . make difficult the isolation of any unified, singular televisual text."[34] In her discussions of the notion of "good" or "quality" TV, however, Charlotte Brunsdon defends retaining the concept of the television text while also taking seriously the difficulties inherent in identifying such an object. She acknowledges a diversity of viewing practices, yet she insists that such strategies can only represent "defining features" of television as a medium "if we choose not to pay attention to what is on the screen."[35] Instead, Brunsdon points to "the symbolic necessity of the audience, its varied inscription throughout the television text," the ways in which "the audience is called on, and constructed by television, as its main source of legitimation" (p. 120). She argues that, far from proving the nonexistence of such a text, critical approaches that focus on the audience or that emphasize television's intertextuality actually prove "that the choice of what is recognized as constituting 'a' text . . . is a political as well as a critical matter" (p. 123). (Thus, for example, critics may attempt to "redeem" an otherwise ideologically suspect media product—Madonna's videos, say, or maternal melodramas—by shifting the focus from the text itself to the various strategies through which viewers construct a preferable reading.)

In claiming that it is not television as a medium, but critical and theoretical approaches *to* television that undermine its textuality, Brunsdon concludes that,

> difficult as it may be, we have to retain a notion of the television text. That is, without the guarantees of common sense or the authority of a political teleology[,] with the recognition of the potentially infinite proliferation of textual sites, and the agency of the always already social reader, in a range of contexts, it is still necessary—and possible—to construct a televisual object of study—and judgment. (P. 125)

However, just as, in Brunsdon's view, soap opera presents a paradigm of television as a whole, so too it offers a particularly extreme demonstration of the difficulty of identifying such an "object of study." There are special problems attendant on defining the soap opera "text," problems that go well beyond the predictable difficulties involved in defining any text—or, indeed, in reaching a critical consensus about the possibility or desirability of identifying "a" text at all. For some, the genre's apparently total lack of closure means that, "[i]n the instance of soap opera, there is no such thing as a text . . . , since the stories in question have no end."[36] While I want to defer my response to this particular characterization until chapter 4, it is by no means the only ground on which critics and theorists deny the existence of the soap opera text. The sheer volume of episodes of an individual television soap opera—the fact that some programs have been broadcast five days a week since the early 1950s—makes it hard for a critic to describe, much less recapture, a program's broadcast history. In contrast, even the longest-running situation comedy or drama, aired only once a week, can more easily be reviewed in its entirety.

In fact, the irretrievability of the complete record of a long-running soap has led Robert Allen and others to claim that such a text can never be defined with any certainty. Allen has argued that there is something about soap opera's narrative form that removes it from the realm of traditional aesthetic objects, making it impossible to describe it as a "text" in any meaningful way. He describes soaps as "narratively anomalous," contending that they "cannot be said to have a 'form' in the traditional sense."[37] Even if we accept the possibility of locating a specific television text, we cannot watch a "complete" soap opera, says Allen, so it is therefore impossible to define it as a text. Significantly, this conclusion is based not only on the predicted lack of series closure—viewers' expectations that an individual program will go on forever—but on the assumption that a particular program's *origins* are also inaccessible:

> I would argue that the soap opera as text can be specified only as the sum of all its episodes broadcast since it began. Hence what we are dealing with is a huge meta-text . . . which [in the case of a 30-year-old program] . . . would take 780 hours . . . to run. . . . But even at the end of this marathon screening, the critic could still not claim to have "read" the entire text of the soap, since during the 32.5 days of continuous viewing, 16 additional hours of textual material would have been produced.[38]

The idea that what Allen calls the soap opera "meta-text" is ultimately irretrievable, however, overlooks several significant factors. First of all, there certainly exist viewers who have experienced the entire broadcast run of particular programs, whether these are older ones who remember *Guiding Light*'s 1952 move to television or viewers who have watched *The Bold and the Beautiful* or *Santa Barbara* since the far more recent beginnings of these shows in the 1980s. Indeed, for some programs, begun in the 1970s or 1980s and canceled within a decade (such as *Ryan's Hope, Generations, Texas, Santa Barbara,* and *Capitol*), there exist viewers who have consumed entire series, from beginning to end. Even if such viewers have missed occasional individual episodes—and in these days of VCRs, we need not assume even that gap—their position would in no way resemble that of Allen's critic, who sits down with a collection of unviewed videotapes representing 30 years of broadcasts. As a matter of fact, we might argue that the viewing experience of Allen's critic would bear so little resemblance to that of a regular viewer as to constitute a different practice entirely, and that it would thus yield few insights into the process by which soaps are actually consumed.

Equally problematic from a theoretical standpoint, however, is the implication that we cannot speak meaningfully about a program as a "text" unless we have consumed it in its entirety. Allen's own work demonstrates that the impossibility of reviewing the entire run of these programs in no way prevents the development of a sophisticated analysis of the form. But even more important, the lack of this kind of total retrievability is part of what marks television's specific difference from print, the medium whose "repeatability" implicitly forms the basis for any theory that presumes the critic must "read" an entire work in order to consider it as a text. Irretrievability also marks television's difference from film, whose discrete individual units—single films—can be endlessly reviewed in a way that television series cannot.[39]

Other differences between television and film or literature also have clear implications for the concept of the TV text, as well as special importance in understanding soap opera. Heath and Skirrow pointed out what is perhaps the most important difference in 1977: Television is characterized by an "immediacy effect . . . supported by the experience of flow: like the world, television never stops, is continuous," and this effect is in turn inflected by "the overall definition of television as 'live.'"[40] Building on this insight, Jane Feuer contends that "notions of 'liveness'" apply as much to taped or filmed and edited programs as they do to events broadcast at the moment of occurrence,[41] and that television's capacity to transmit events as they happen has led to the application of "an ideology of the live" (p. 14) to all television transmissions—regardless of the actual temporal relationship between an event and its televisual presentation. Thus all television transmissions are in some sense presented, consumed, and understood as if they were live.

The concept of television's perpetual liveness will come up again in connection with soap operas' multiple weekly installments, but for now I want to underline the fact that this "liveness" is at the root of some of TV's central differences from film. Feuer points to the conflation of the "live" with the "real"—if something is happening as we watch it, it must "really" be happening—as well as to the way that television seems "real" in the sense of being "an entirely ordinary experience" (p. 15). She also emphasizes the processes by which the "circuit of address" on genuinely live programs "propagates an ideology of 'liveness' overcoming [the] fragmentation" of television's ordinary segmented flow (p. 17). These observations have special meaning in the case of soap operas, where the apparent liveness of television is augmented by the programs' manipulation of time. By promoting the fiction that viewers' and characters' time passes at the same rate, soaps present themselves as "real" in both of the senses Feuer employs. The fact that many soap opera events take the same amount of time they would occupy in viewers' lives makes their depictions especially "realistic," while the frequent coincidence between "real time" and both diegetic time and the time that elapses between episodes lends an air of immediacy to events within the programs.[42]

These differences between television and film or literature suggest that soap operas, which exemplify so many television traits, may demand an entirely new conception of "text," one that allows for the kind of viewing habits that actually characterize the experience of their regular audience members. In this connection, the notion of soaps as an "indefinitely expandable middle"[43] may be useful, although that notion's usual association with the programs' lack of closure will become problematic in chapter 4. Putting aside for the moment, however, the question of whether or not soap operas ever achieve closure, viewers' consumption of them certainly has an identifiable beginning. Regardless of whether or not that beginning coincides with the first broadcast episode of the program, it constitutes the beginning of the viewing experience, and thus a point that we can at least provisionally identify as the beginning of a text.

Audience research suggests, in fact, that viewers think of the soap opera "text" in just this way. Ellen Seiter and her colleagues, for instance, have noted that their "informants were aware of the impossibility for a single person to grasp fully the text of a soap opera," largely because they could not watch every single episode.[44] Nevertheless, these same viewers assembled "a condensed version of the text" through selective viewing, consultation with other viewers, and speculation based on their own "expert textual knowledge" (p. 234). The authors therefore "identified the text with the experience of soap operas as our viewers described it on the basis of their individual exposure to the genre" (p. 232).

Clearly, however, there is more at stake here than questions about whether or not one can define a program without seeing it from its beginning to its end. Allen's concern over the impossibility of reviewing the complete broadcast history of a particular soap opera, for example, is ultimately based on a critique of the very notion of genre. Rather than defining soap opera in traditional generic terms, he prefers to consider it as the intersection of the three different discursive systems used by the industrial, critical, and viewer communities.[45]

Yet it is not necessary, as Allen seems to imply, to choose between rigid genre categories and no genres at all. Instead, we can follow theorists like Steve Neale, who understands genres as "systems of expectation and hypothesis," as processes that involve both producers and consumers of the programs that comprise them.[46] This is particularly appropriate in the case of soap operas, for, as audience studies have demonstrated, regular viewers bring very specific kinds of expectations to their viewing experience. While they may not talk explicitly about soap operas or soap-opera-like programs in terms of genre, they understand the series they watch as following a set of dramatic, narrative, ideological, and moral rules and conventions in which certain sorts of developments are permitted and others are unlikely or impossible.[47] Throughout this book, I will be arguing that this is actually a crucial component of audience pleasure, and that competent soap viewers play a constant game of speculation and anticipation with regard to future story and character development. In a form whose viewers often draw on years of detailed expertise regarding specific programs and soap operas in general, the relevance of an understanding of genre as a relationship between producers' texts and consumers' expectations seems clear.

Let me return now to the definition I proposed at the beginning of this chapter:

> A soap opera is a continuing fictional dramatic television program, presented in multiple serial installments each week through a narrative composed of interlocking storylines that focus on the relationships within a specific community of characters.

As I have already indicated, each element in this definition can be found in other categories of contemporary U.S. television, and any regular TV viewer will be able to name programs that are not soap operas but that still incorporate many of these same traits. The serial format, for example, characterizes *Hill Street Blues*, *St. Elsewhere*, *L.A. Law*, *Wiseguy*, *Dallas*, *Dynasty*, *Knots Landing*, and, through the use of multipart story arcs and cliffhanger episodes, certain situation comedies as well (e.g., *Cheers*, *Murphy Brown*). Multiple and often interlocking storylines are a major structural feature, not only of the dramatic programs I've listed, but of *Hotel*, *Fantasy Island*, and *The Love Boat* as well. Personal relationships within a self-contained community dominate shows like *Northern Exposure* and *thirtysomething*, as well as more traditional series, such as *The Andy Griffith Show*, *M*A*S*H*, and *Emergency*.

Despite their individual appearance across a range of genres, however, certain of these characteristics are firmly associated with soap operas: Any program that presents an intense mesh of personal stories that continue, serial-like, beyond a single episode, is likely to be called a soap. While the term has long been used as a sweeping derogatory equivalent for "trash TV" or "melodrama," it is now broadly applied not only by cultural critics, but by journalists and even industry promotion departments, and no longer inevitably signals a specific negative evaluation of an individual program.[48] But it is this specific *combination* of characteristics, the idiosyncratic mix of these familiar elements that distinguishes a soap from a program that simply employs some of them. As Stephen Neale writes, "Generic specificity is a question not of particular and exclusive elements, however defined, but of exclusive and particular combinations and articulations of elements."[49]

In order to understand how these characteristics combine to create a unique television genre, then, let us look at the elements individually. *A soap opera is a continuing fictional dramatic television program*: By using the word "continuing," I mean to distinguish soaps, which are presented as first-run episodes 52 weeks a year, from the more limited runs of conventional television series aired according to industry "seasons," as well as from shorter miniseries, multipart made-for-television movies, and so on. (Thus, while sharing many traits with U.S. soaps, the *telenovelas* of Latin America do not qualify as continuing dramas in this sense, since they usually have a limited, if lengthy, run.)

Soap operas' fictional status may seem self-evident, but the May 1992 debut of MTV's nonfiction series *The Real World*—described in its own network promotions as "a real-life soap opera"—suggests otherwise. We need to be careful to distinguish fictional television programs from those that are unscripted and may be "performed" by nonactors, as in the case of *The Real World* and its precursors, the 1973 PBS series *An American Family* and Fox's 1991 *Yearbook*. Although such programs are elaborately mediated and constructed through highly selective editing and other practices, their allegedly nonfictional status puts them into a different category of television genres.

I also distinguish dramatic from possible comedy and parody series—*Soap* and *Mary Hartman, Mary Hartman*, for instance—to emphasize the fact that, while soap opera performance may involve a high degree of self-consciousness and may even be overtly camp, the programs themselves are essentially unironic. While it was possible to follow the storylines of *Soap* or *Mary Hartman* as one would a traditional serial, both programs offered preferred readings of themselves as parodies.[50] Soap operas, on the other hand, take themselves and their conventions seriously; indeed, it is that very seriousness that permits certain audiences to perform what Jane Feuer has called "camp decodings" of the programs and that makes possible the parodies that represent the ultimate ironic reading of them.[51] While Feuer insists that the decodings performed by gay male viewers are actually among *Dynasty*'s preferred readings, I am obviously suggesting just the opposite: that they exist in contrast to the dominant readings proposed by the program itself. It may also be true, however, that prime-time serials such as *Dynasty* offer, or at the very least make space for, easily accessible alternative, oppositional, camp, and/or comic readings as a function of their attempt to appeal to the broadest possible audience—a goal that characterizes U.S. prime-time far more than daytime television.

According to my definition, soaps are presented in *multiple installments each week*; in the United States, that means five days a week. Although many elements separate daytime from so-called "prime-time soaps"—including the prime-time emphasis on business and financial power—in my view these are secondary to the far more basic differences that arise from five-day-a-week versus weekly broadcast. In fact, what we might call soaps' "dailiness" has significant consequences both for the programs' structure and style and for regular viewers' experience of them.

Early theorists like Tania Modleski argued that the specific narrative structure of soap operas, particularly their cycles of interruption and repetition, closely resembles the daily lives of conventional housewives and therefore makes the experience of watching soap operas especially appealing, as well as easy to reconcile with the interruptions that supposedly characterize their days.[52] Others have contended that it is the domestic content of the programs that makes soaps both interesting and relevant to women viewers whose attention is traditionally focused on the personal.[53]

I would argue, however, that the intimacy that seems to characterize the experience of watching soap operas results at least as much from viewers' daily exposure to the programs as it does from the specific content and structure of the episodes themselves, or from particular camera work and other production choices.[54] The relatively brief interval between episodes permits the act of watching them to become part of a regular routine—part of "viewers' daily rituals"[55]—constructing a uniquely intense viewing experience and investing it with a status quite different from that of programs consumed weekly or even less frequently. While audience studies acknowledge that many fans miss occasional episodes or even watch irregularly, the same research suggests that they also watch with the assumption that daily viewing of the programs is the ideal.[56]

"Dailiness" functions on the levels of both production and consumption, and is connected to the "ideology of liveness" that has dominated and defined U.S. (and British) television from the outset. As Jane Feuer indicates in regard to *Good Morning America*, the construction of liveness, whether actual or artificial, allows a particular program "to insinuate itself into our lives."[57] Habitual daily viewing intensifies this process in the case of soap operas, and the notion of *repetition* may be useful in beginning to understand why. Charlotte Brunsdon has pointed out that, while researchers have concentrated on the consequences of the fact that women often watch soap operas in groups, a more thorough understanding may come from work that distinguishes "between modes of viewing which are repeated on a regular basis and uncommon or unfamiliar modes of viewing."[58] This seems to me to point to a potentially crucial way of understanding the television viewing experience. Although many recent theorists have called attention to television's penchant for repetition, it has often been made secondary to the notion of interruption, as in John Caughie's claim that, like the "novelistic" in general, "the television novelistic is organized around interruption."[59] Caughie makes this point as a way of linking television to a long narrative tradition, to which television's "definitive contribution" is the development of "a narrative form built on the principle of interruption and therefore organizing expectation and attention to the short segments which will soften the disruption of being interrupted."[60]

But while it is important to consider the narrative effect of the constant interruption that characterizes commercial television, an argument like Caughie's ignores viewers' habit of returning to these "interrupted" television narratives on a weekly or, in the case of soaps, daily basis. The experience of watching an individual television program may indeed be marked by disruption, as the episode's forward movement is repeatedly broken by the intrusion of commercials and other forms of promotion, and Raymond Williams's notion of "flow" captures the extent to which an evening of viewing can be seen as consisting of a loose assembly of such fragments. But if we step back to take a wider perspective of, say, a week, a month, or a year of viewing, we can also see a pattern of repetition in which much of the audience returns again and again, not only to specific programs, but to particular day-parts (such as early morning or prime-time). As Heath and Skirrow maintain in their revision of Williams, "the 'central fact of television experience' is much less flow than *flow and regularity*; the anachronistic succession is also a constant repetition."[61]

Although nonfiction genres like talk, news, or game shows may operate on a similar schedule, soap operas are the only *fictional* examples of first-run daily telecast on U.S. television. This therefore puts soaps in a unique position as paradigmatic, not simply of the extent to which television narrative is built on constant interruption, but of the concomitant expectation that the interrupted narrative will resume. Indeed, as I will argue shortly, each soap opera episode presents in miniature both the "flow" and the pattern of return typical of television.

One question raised by my insistence on multiple weekly installments as a defining characteristic of soap opera is whether some threshold number of episodes must air each week in order for a program to qualify as a soap. For instance, in contrast to the U.S. standard of five episodes per week, British serials such as *Coronation Street* and *EastEnders* broadcast only two or three, usually with an omnibus installment on the weekend. The question of how these programs' multiple episodes fit into my definition is here complicated by the fact that, while U.S. daytime TV serials have always aired five days a week and had completely replaced radio serials by the 1960–61 season, their British television counterparts have had a far more varied broadcast history, including the fact that radio serials still continue to air alongside them. Thus, although the expectations and consumption patterns of U.S. soap opera viewers have been shaped by the kind of "dailiness" I am describing, British viewers may have quite a different set of expectations. Similarly, from the production side, U.S. soaps are inevitably structured around the demands of five-day-a-week broadcast, while the narrative and story development of British programs may be organized to meet quite different demands.[62]

These differences remind us of the crucial role played by local viewing (and production) conditions. As Sean Cubitt points out in his book on video culture, "the importance of the local . . . helps to circumscribe the generalisation of arguments to universal values, geographically or historically. . . . Programmes or programme formats in world-wide distribution are viewed differently in various cultures, even within the same culture, or by the same person viewing at different times."[63] Cubitt is arguing here that, while the widespread use of VCRs has changed British viewing habits in fundamental ways, the fact that communal, real-time viewing still dominates in many other parts of the world makes it difficult to extrapolate from British experience to the experience of viewers elsewhere. But his remarks are relevant for all areas of TV, including the exportation of the U.S. soap opera format (and of actual programs) to other cultures. Despite a shared set of televisual conventions and the long-standing exchange of specific individual programs, both the production and the consumption conditions of British and U.S. television differ considerably.[64] (Among the most obvious and influential differences is the historical development of U.S. television as primarily commercial and privately owned, versus the British model of noncommercial government monopoly.)[65] Thus, while the overlap between the two systems allows us to use examples from one to illuminate the other, we must do so with great care, for conclusions based on the experience of U.S. television may not apply smoothly to the British, and vice versa.

The emphasis on multiple episodes provides a perfect example of the complications that may arise when we ignore the differences between television cultures, not least because an individual program acquires its significance within the context of the larger televisual landscape. Five-day-a-week U.S. programs such as soap operas are explicitly marked as different from weekly ones, and watching them is therefore necessarily a different experience from watching those that appear once a week. Since U.S. television currently has no programs scheduled to air two or three times a week, the primary differences are between five-day-a-week and weekly broadcast. (I am speaking here of first-run episodes, rather than programs that are scheduled for one original and one or more repeat airings during a single week— a common practice on many local PBS affiliates, as well as on MTV, CNN, HBO, and other cable services.) In the United Kingdom, however, where programs may air anywhere from daily to weekly, the difference is somewhat more complicated. We might argue, therefore, that, in any television system that relies mainly on a *weekly* programming rotation, it is the experience of *multiple* episodes during a single week that is marked as different and therefore significant. Thus, the British practice of airing, say, three weekly episodes of a serial would generate many of the same patterns of expectation, including an incorporation of a particular series into viewers' regular routines similar to that generated by the five-day-a-week broadcast of U.S. soap operas.[66]

My emphasis on "dailiness" also raises an interesting question about another category of programs, series that are "stripped," or aired five or even seven days a week through syndication: Can a series designed to run weekly "become" a soap opera simply by moving into five-day-a-week syndication? In most cases the answer is no, since a sitcom or a traditional crime drama stripped daily still fails to meet the other criteria that define a soap opera. But the situation alters considerably when we consider dramas that closely resemble soaps in their use of interlocking storylines and their emphasis on personal relationships. Series such as *thirtysomething* and *L.A. Law*, which focus on the relationships within a small, essentially closed group of friends and relatives or coworkers, beg for comparison with soap operas. *L.A. Law*'s tendency to leave problems unresolved at the end of an episode and *thirtysomething*'s obsession with questions of gender, romance, and family, as well as the degree of viewers' emotional involvement with both series and their characters, make it particularly tempting to classify them as soaps.[67]

I have been arguing that, among other things, daily viewing allows audience members to incorporate a program into their lives in a way quite different from programs that recur on a weekly basis. If I am correct about this effect, then the intensity and intimacy created by daily involvement with a dramatic series does not depend on the specific structure of the narrative itself. Nor is it dependent on the particular purpose—daytime or prime-time scheduling, weekly or daily rotation, broadcast or cable setting, domestic or foreign consumption—for which it was originally designed. But the fact that I have been invoking the concept of "dailiness" primarily in terms of its effect on viewers does not mean that the prospect of five-day-a-week broadcast has no influence on story development, narrative structure, characterization, or other features of the production.

For instance, writers, directors, actors, and other participants in the production process who have five days a week in which to develop a story, explore a character, express an idea, consider a social issue, and so on, can employ a degree of detail unavailable to those who produce a weekly series. Soap opera stories proceed at what inexperienced viewers may see as an excruciating pace, but because of its attempt to imitate the rate at which events transpire in "real life," this pace contributes to the fiction of the programs' "liveness," the sense that the events depicted are actually happening as we watch them. Once again, the phenomenon of "dailiness" and television's "ideology of liveness" inflect each other through soaps' construction of time.

There are also specific negative consequences for production and performance style. Soaps' year-round five-day-a-week broadcast schedule requires a five-day-a-week production schedule, which means that actors have limited rehearsal time. This in turn results in what many viewers recognize as characteristically unpolished performances, exacerbated by a limited use of retakes, along with editing and production values that tend to be judged by nonfans as considerably "lower" than the more lavish ones of most prime-time television. In some ways, the fact that actors flub lines or improvise when memory fails them may contribute to soaps' apparent realism, since characters' conversations often seem no smoother than viewers'. At the same time, however, the impossibility of creating the perfect performances and camera work typical of prime-time programs also contributes to the low esteem in which nonfans hold soap operas.

If we were to arrange TV dramas along a continuum ordered in terms of their increasing likeness to soap opera—with, say, completely freestanding episodic series at one end and prime-time serials at the other—and then consider the impact of daily cable- or broadcast on each of them, we would find that, by the time we got to the daily syndicated airing of a series like *Dallas*, we would have reached a viewing experience nearly indistinguishable from that of a "real" soap. The possibility that a series originally designed as a weekly prime-time drama can seemingly be transformed into a soap opera also serves as yet another reminder of the importance of developing a comprehensive definition of the genre. In this case, soaps can be distinguished from other programs that might air daily by the fact that they take *serial form* and are generally characterized by episodic nonclosure, which manifests itself through the postponement of individual storyline resolutions and the use of major and minor cliff-hangers in place of the more definitive conclusions typical of traditional episodic television.[68] John Ellis claims that the serial form is actually characteristic of television narratives of all sorts, including episodic series, in which the essential problematic that powers a program remains unresolved across episodes.[69] Precisely because this brings us back once again to the idea that television is marked overall as much by repetition and return as by interruption, we need to be careful to distinguish between true serial form and the "serialness" of TV in general.[70]

This open-endedness is one of the most discussed aspects of soap operas' narrative form, forming the basis for many theories about soaps' narrative structure. Some theorists have discerned ties between irresolution and a specific kind of female viewing pleasure, while others have argued that nonclosure undermines the traditional narrative trajectory. Soap opera closure is a complex issue, and I will argue in chapter 4 that, while soaps do not attain traditional narrative closure at many levels—both at the levels of individual episodes and, as a rule, at the level of the program as a whole—they do achieve it in a number of other important ways. In addition, occasional individual episodes actually end with the explicit resolution of a specific problem, often a question of identity, and thus resemble a traditional television episode.

Still, there can be no doubt about their basic serial nature, an element that, as Robert Allen and others have documented, has its roots in the form's commercial origins. And like the airing of multiple episodes each week, soaps' serial format enhances the ease with which viewers can incorporate the programs into their regular routines. As Christine Gledhill contends, seriality is an "initially accidental but ultimately defining feature," one that lends "solidity" and "three dimensional reality to a tale that runs in parallel to its [viewers'] lives."[71]

Closely connected to their serial nature is the fact that soap operas' narrative is composed of multiple, *interlocking storylines*. The adaptation of the form from radio to television and the shift over the years from 15- to 30- and then to 60-minute episodes allowed storylines to multiply from the two or three that characterized radio and early television serials to the dozen or more ongoing stories that can be found in current programs. In contrast to more conventional storytelling practice, however, soap operas have from their beginnings featured plural storylines, and this has had a very specific consequence for their narrative development. Rather than following the linear path of a single story, organized around the exploits of a single (heroic) character, soap opera narratives necessarily proceed in what is at most only a quasi-linear fashion, with each story's forward progress constantly interrupted by the eruption of the latest events in another one. Typically, programs will cut among three stories in a single episode, allotting each only one scene at a time before moving on to another story. This means that soap operas offer an extremely complex form of storytelling, one that requires viewers to follow several stories at once and to suspend their interest in one temporarily when events from another intervene.[72]

As I suggested earlier, however, the multiplicity of soap opera storylines also imitates the "flow" of (commercial U.S.) television itself, in which regularly recurring programs constantly interrupt each other. In a week in which a habitual *Roseanne* viewer watches only a few other prime-time programs, for instance, she may be required to remember what distinguishes the individual members of the Conner family from one another, while paying equal attention to the intervening episodes of *Melrose Place, Seinfeld, Murphy Brown,* and *NYPD Blue,* and trying all the while not to be distracted by ads for a variety of products, as well as promotions for programs in which she has no interest. In the case of soap operas, of course, these interventions occur *within* as well as *between* individual episodes, and while an hour-long episode typically features events from only three or four storylines, a typical week may present developments in three or four times as many, most of which in turn assume viewer memories of earlier stories. Once again, then, soaps can be seen as a paradigm of U.S. television's overall form, making precision about their operations even more important.

Each story's indirect movement toward a climax or resolution is further complicated by the fact that individual soap opera storylines are all in some way connected to one another. That is because, to return to my definition, all of them *focus on the relationships within a specific community of characters.* We will see in chapter 3 that the construction of this community plays a crucial role in the organization of soap opera narrative, particularly in the programs' obsession with characters' exchange of private information. But for the moment, the important fact is that soaps take place within closed communities and that they emphasize the personal relationships among members of those communities rather than, for instance, their political or work lives, or the connection between a particular community and the larger world.

Such overlap between characters' lives and among the storylines that depict them must be distinguished, however, from what occurs on a program in which multiple storylines are linked merely by the fact that their protagonists share a law partnership or cruise-line employment. Although individual *L.A. Law* or *Love Boat* storylines may resonate with each other, for example, developments within each of them tend to be relatively autonomous.[73] In contrast, soap opera characters are diegetically entangled by their past, present, and potential future ties of kinship and romance, blood, marriage, and friendship. They are narratively entangled by the fact that their economic, political, and other "public" relationships are subordinated to these personal ties. Thus, the intimate connections among soap opera characters mean that events in one storyline inevitably have consequences in others.

The domestic, personal, and emotional emphasis of soap opera has received a considerable amount of critical and theoretical attention, most of it attributing the programs' focus to the fact that the form was designed—and still functions—to target a predominantly female audience, presumed to be interested in personal relations. Subsequent chapters of this book will take up many of the ways in which soap opera expresses what Charlotte Brunsdon has identified as the "ideological problematic" of the genre, "personal life in its everyday realization through personal relationships."[74] For the moment, however, I simply want to point out the necessity of understanding this interest in the personal as a defining characteristic of the genre. Although the melodramatic strategies increasingly being adopted by U.S. television have given the personal a new prominence across genres, it is important to distinguish here between, for example, police or medical stories framed in personal terms and dramas that have the personal as their primary obsession. On a melodrama-inflected series like *Hill Street Blues* or *NYPD Blue*, for instance, major storylines about crime are often framed by the personal concerns of the police officers (or, less frequently, the criminals or lawyers) involved, but the relationships among characters, their positions within the program, and the implications of individual story resolutions are couched primarily in terms of public issues such as the crumbling criminal justice system. In contrast, on a soap like *Another World*, which regularly features storylines about crime, the "public" aspects of such stories are subordinated to the personal by being couched

almost entirely in terms of the familial, romantic, and emotional relationships between characters. And while those characters may have
other ties, they are connected to each other primarily by personal
rather than public bonds.

My definition omits a number of characteristics that are commonly considered to be central to soap opera narrative and style. The
major missing element, of course, is nonclosure, but other traits of
narrative, production, and performance style have also figured prominently in critics' attempts to outline what constitutes a soap opera. I
do not mean to suggest, however, that the nonlinear narrative strategies that advance soap operas' interlocking storylines are unimpor-
tant, but instead that their nonlinearity is a function of the fact that
they are intertwined in such a complex manner. Nor would I claim
that the programs' almost exclusive use of interior sets, their obsession with close-ups, their glossy "look," and the cosmetic, costum-
ing, and decorative excesses usually associated with current soap opera production are trivial factors in constructing a soap's televisual
style. What I do want to argue is that these are not necessary characteristics of the genre, but rather, stylistic elements that *serve* soap
opera structure and format rather than *defining* them. The distinction I am drawing here is between those elements that define soap
opera as a genre and the characteristics that merely mark them, a
category that also includes what Robert Allen has called their
"subliterary" production features, such as authorial anonymity and
"industrial assembly-line methods."[75]

Some of these elements are more easily identified as secondary
than others. As proof of the dispensability of the current "look," for
example, we need only turn to programs from the days of black-and-
white broadcast. Early episodes look grim and dowdy in comparison
to today's colorful glossiness, yet no one would seriously claim that
their lack of high-fashion glitz means that the 1950s or 1960s incar-
nations are not "really" soaps. British serials' focus on working-class
life and the obvious "ordinariness" of their mise-en-scène also suggest how wide a range of "looks" might be possible within the genre.
At the same time, the fact that genres like the variety, talk, and game
show—and to some extent the whole range of current U.S. prime-
time programming—are characterized by glamorous costumes, im-

plausible hairstyles, and elaborate sets should demonstrate that excessive style alone is not enough to make a program a soap opera. Similarly, a serious consideration of the whole range of programming available on U.S. TV reveals that the specific settings (domestic interiors) and camera work (close-ups) familiar to soap opera viewers actually characterize many genres. Situation comedies, for example, tend both to take place in the home or workplace and to employ a limited number of indoor sets, just as soap operas do. While primetime family dramas (*Family, The Waltons, Little House on the Prairie*) make more frequent and more sophisticated use of outdoor locations, they, too, tend to share with soaps a focus on domestic settings. So, too, the intense close-ups that seem to provide soap opera viewers with such intimate knowledge of individual characters' affective lives serve the same function in a variety of film and television genres. Soap operas may rely more heavily on such shots, but the practice was well-established long before the rise of television.[76]

Among the other major features with a claim to defining status, some writers have identified soaps' emphasis on dialogue over action. Christine Gledhill, for instance, claims that "[s]oap opera constructs a feminine world of personal conversation," while Robert Allen describes soaps as "in a sense, 'about' talk."[77] There is certainly no doubt that soap opera narrative moves forward more through the discussion of events than through their direct on-screen representation, yet I have chosen not to identify this as a basic defining trait because I think it has more to do with the *content* of the programs than with their essential form. That is, I see the primacy of talk, the telling and retelling of stories, as a function of the programs' concentration on personal relationships and their continual efforts to construct a particular kind of community. (I will return to the question of soap talk in chapter 3, which deals with the ways in which soap characters' compulsive discussions work to erase conventional boundaries between private and public experience.)

Another characteristic of soap operas that may seem essential to the genre is its commercially motivated targeting of a predominantly female audience. As Allen and others have shown, the form originated in advertisers' desire to reach women consumers, making soap operas perhaps the most transparently commercial of all broadcast genres.[78] But the fact that commercial radio and television exist primarily to deliver audiences to advertisers means that the genre's history is not unique, but merely extreme. Furthermore, television producers' practice of aiming specific programming at increasingly narrow demographic groups means that soap operas are only one among many genres and subgenres designed for a specialized audience. Adult women are extremely desirable viewers because of their control of household purchasing power, and in recent years we have seen their importance acknowledged by network programming strategies such as CBS's famous Monday night lineup of "women's" shows, rooted initially in a desire to attract female viewers uninterested in ABC's *Monday Night Football.* The success of that strategy has reinforced faith in what has come to be called "boutique" programming, to the point where some network executives have begun to dismiss the traditional race to be number one in the overall ratings, insisting instead on the greater significance of high ratings among "quality" viewers. At the same time, increasing pressure from cablecasters, Fox Broadcasting, and the videocassette market has made the targeting of reliable, if small, audiences a standard television practice, particularly among beleagured Big Three network programmers.[79]

A genre definition that assumed women as the primary audience would also forestall the possibility of soap operas designed to be watched by other target audiences. Yet there is reason to believe that many other potential soap opera audiences exist, such as the ones for which *Swans Crossing* and *Paradise Beach*—nationally syndicated five-day-a-week serials launched, respectively, in June 1992 and June 1993 and aimed at teens and preteens of both sexes—were designed. Serials have also been developed in college video production classes, on community-access cable stations, and elsewhere, often with fairly specific audiences (students, gay and lesbian viewers) in mind, and it is easy to imagine projects aimed at other population groups or subcultures. Although soap operas have traditionally been a "women's genre," we do not need to assume that genre rules demand that soap operas be aimed at women.

Still, I agree with Charlotte Brunsdon's argument that the cultural competence required to make sense of soap operas consists, not merely of experience of the television genre, but of a particular kind of social knowledge. Writing of the British serial *Crossroads*, Brunsdon has maintained that the program—and, by implication, the genre as a whole—"textually implies a feminine viewer to the extent that its textual discontinuities, in order to make sense, require a viewer competent within the ideological and moral frameworks (the rules) of romance, marriage and family life."[80] Although conceived in a British setting, her words apply equally to the U.S. context, but it is crucial to recognize that she is using the notion of a "feminine viewer" to represent, not a biological female or even a gendered female social subject, but a set of knowledges and skills normally associated with women in patriarchal culture. Only if we understand the "feminine viewer" in these terms is it reasonable to identify the soap opera audience as *necessarily* "female."[81]

Annette Kuhn has pointed out the importance of distinguishing between *spectators*—the viewing subjects "constituted in signification, interpellated by the . . . TV text"[82]—and the actual *social audiences* that consume particular texts. Although Kuhn regards both of these groups as primarily discursive concepts, her terms are still helpful in separating the audiences targeted by, say, a particular soap opera producer from the viewers who actually watch that program. Still, I also have not included as a defining characteristic of the genre the fact that, to some extent apart from industry and advertiser intentions, soap opera audiences are in fact predominantly female. Ratings demonstrate gender differences in viewing across television genres, often corresponding to the most stereotypical ideas of what interests women and men.[83] Thus, to affirm soap operas' uniqueness on the grounds that they offer a special viewing opportunity for women is to overlook the fact that, at least in the United States, differences in viewing habits are quite often defined by gender.[84]

Finally, I have another reason for not defining the genre primarily in terms of who consumes it. Because viewing patterns may change over time (for instance, more men now watch daytime soap operas than did during, say, the 1950s and 1960s), a definition that depended on the identity of current viewers would be inherently unstable. For many theorists, this very instability would be an advantage, reflecting the inherent instability of the television text and underlining the role viewers play in constructing the programs they consume, and therefore in defining specific TV genres. But as I indicated in my introduction, I am drawing on a different notion of the viewing process, one that depends at least as much on the existence of an identifiable, if difficult to describe, television text as it does on view-ers' active participation in the construction of that text. While I will return throughout the following chapters to the ways in which view-ers—particularly women—make sense of soap opera, my attention will be focused, as theirs is, on the television screen.

3

Public Exposure: Privacy and the Construction of the Soap Opera Community

> The protagonist, with whom our sympathy and understanding lie, is subjected to the curious and prurient gaze of intrusive community, neighbours, friends and family so that the spectator's own look becomes self-conscious and awkward.
>
> —Laura Mulvey, "Melodrama Inside and Outside the Home"

> You can't keep any secrets at the brownstone.
>
> —Frisco Jones, *General Hospital*

■ Having proposed soap opera's interest in relations within a fictional community as a defining characteristic of the genre, I might next logically ask: what sort of relationships within exactly what kind of community? The idea that soap operas bring the domestic sphere into public view is hardly a new one. In soaps, writes Dennis Porter, "the private sphere of intimate relations . . . remains magically open to the viewer."[1] Indeed, most feminist analyses see this revelation of the personal as providing one of the genre's main appeals for women. In Charlotte Brunsdon's words, "The ideological problematic of soap opera—the frame or field in which meanings are made, in which significance is constructed narratively—is that of 'personal life.'. . . [T]he action of soap opera . . . *colonizes* the public masculine sphere. . . . It is through the concerns and values of the personal sphere that the public sphere is represented."[2]

As feminist theorists have long made clear, our contemporary understanding of the notions of public and private have been profoundly influenced by the concept of separate male and female spheres. This doctrine, which links men with the social, economic, and political world outside the home and women with private, domestic concerns, has manifested itself in many different, often contradictory ways over the last two centuries, from outright prohibitions on women's participation in such "public" activities as education and politics to the strategic redefinition of teaching and social work as essentially "domestic" tasks.[3] Despite such changes in their precise contents, however, the categories of separate, gendered spheres have remained steady. Indeed, certain aspects—the association of women with child rearing and housework and of men with economic concerns—have been so powerful that they have shaped our most basic understanding of what it means to be a male or a female citizen, leading theorists like Nancy Fraser to call the entire notion of separate spheres "an institutional arrangement that is . . . one, if not the, linchpin of modern women's subordination."[4]

Along with this association, however, goes another one that has particular significance for our analysis of soap opera community life: the idea, dominant under the sociocultural arrangements of capitalist patriarchy, that "[d]omestic institutions depoliticize certain matters by personalizing . . . them; they cast these as private-domestic or personal-familial matters in contradistinction to public, political matters."[5] The dominant ideology of Western culture thus insists that a rigid (but natural, inevitable) separation exists between private concerns—family, romance, sexuality, housework, personal taste—and their public counterparts. As a result, then, feminists, gay men and lesbians, and others who declare that social change is necessary in order to alter the terms on which personal life is lived are marked as (inappropriately) politicizing an otherwise apolitical personal sphere.

From the perspective of those seeking change, of course, things are considerably more complex. To begin with, as Bruce Robbins writes, "no sites are inherently or eternally public."[6] Further, it is not always even clear whether the obliteration or the preservation of privacy is the worthier feminist goal.[7]

I want to introduce the soap opera into the midst of this debate because the genre calls into question just what constitutes public and private behavior.[8] While the critical emphasis has largely been on the way that the programs personalize the public sphere, however, I want to make a somewhat different argument: that soap operas actually *redefine* both the public and private spheres, specifically through their treatment of the concept of privacy. Soap opera characters conduct their lives in physical settings whose public and communal nature ultimately makes privacy impossible, and this in turn works to construct a fictional community whose members have an unrestricted right of access to each other's most personal experiences and feelings. In effect, there is no "private" sphere in the soap opera community because there is no privacy.

Although privacy and its violation play a part in many fictional forms, they are central to soap opera narrative. In fact, the genre admits of no significant distinction between things that are kept private and those that are exposed to public knowledge. Or rather, while the distinction exists, the barrier which in daily life permits—or forces—people to separate "private" and "public" experiences, and to keep the former to themselves and their intimates, is breached regularly *in* and *by* the soap opera narrative. I will argue in this chapter that the public exposure of private feelings and experiences is actually the ruling dynamic of soap operas, established through the setting of characters' lives in highly public situations and perpetuated by their utter inability to say and mean the simple words, "It's none of your business." In the soap opera world, everything is *everyone's* business.

This collapse of the private into the public is, as Mimi White has remarked in another context, "at once the subject of programming and its mode of narrativization."[9] While the genre's uninhibited exposure of intimate information might tempt psychoanalytically inspired theorists to characterize the soap opera narrative as hysterical, however, it is quite different from what Patrice Petro has characterized as the "hysterical" text, which "might be said to hold a 'secret' of which it is unaware."[10] The soap opera text is all too aware of the secrets it holds; indeed, it might be said to speak about them all the time.

Such "speaking" occurs at both the televisual and the diegetic levels, both to viewers and between characters. The spectacle of soap opera thus consists of the display *to the viewer* of scenes of great intimacy, and of characters revealing and exchanging private or secret information.[11] If Dennis Porter's well-known formulation about the close-up is true—that "[a] face in close-up is what before the age of film only a lover or a mother ever saw"[12]—it is equally true that soap operas offer us the regular sight of intimacies formerly visible only to the voyeur, the sound of words previously audible only to the eavesdropper.

It has now become commonplace, of course, to characterize television in terms of its "domesticity." Analysts as theoretically disparate as John Ellis and Lynne Joyrich invoke this association, Ellis calling broadcast television "a profoundly domestic phenomenon" and Joyrich describing the medium as "[t]ruly a 'family affair,' [in which] the familial defines not only the medium's preferred subject matter, but also the structure of both its time flow and mode of address, and TV's central position within domestic space strengthens just this association."[13] But while such arguments bolster the recognition of soap opera as television's paradigmatic genre, I am talking here about something more than this apparent "domesticity." And while soaps actually enact their exposure of private life in as simple and direct a way as publicly airing scenes of home, I am also referring to something beyond the mere televisual depiction of domestic life. Other genres—not least, the domestic sitcom—take private life, family, and the home as their primary subjects; in fact, as Lynn Spigel has documented, the melding of domestic and public life is central to the history of television itself, which was originally situated in just those terms.[14]

Let me begin, then, by considering the programs' specific diegetic techniques, the ways in which individual characters' privacy is habitually obliterated within the soap opera narrative through the exposure to other characters of various bits of intimate information: the identities of lovers, the nature of deeply held feelings or opinions, the truth about past experiences or future plans. This violation of privacy plays a crucial role in defining and constructing the fictional community within which soap opera events occur, and its fundamental mechanism is the placement of soap opera characters in locales that lack even elementary forms of privacy. They rent rooms in boardinghouses with common living rooms and kitchens or dwell in multigenerational family groups, work in buildings with open lounges, eat and drink in busy bars and restaurants, and socialize at large public gatherings. Because they spend nearly all of their time in such spaces, they must conduct their most private business essentially in public, pursuing clandestine relationships in the town's most popular night-spot, exchanging secret information in the hospital lounge, confronting deceitful spouses at the holiday ball. Even more important, locations that are conventionally seen as private, such as the home, are redefined on soap operas as public space.

Viewers will be able to list examples of these settings from any soap with which they are familiar. If we count only core characters' primary residences and the shows' largest employers, for example, CBS's *The Young and the Restless* offers, at a minimum, Jabot Cosmetics and Newman Enterprises, where many characters work; the Newman ranch, sometime residence of Victor Newman, his wife, their children, her second husband, and several long-term guests, including a man thought to be Victor's illegitimate son; and the Abbott family home, the residence at various times of miscellaneous Abbotts, their romantic partners, spouses, ex-spouses, children, employees— and even, at one point, the niece of the Abbotts' devoted housekeeper. ABC's *All My Children* features the Cortlandt, Chandler, and Tyler mansions, Pine Valley Hospital, the Valley Inn, and Myrtle Fargate's boardinghouse, while *One Life to Live* includes the Llanview hospital, the *Banner* newspaper offices, the Lord/Riley family manor Llanfair, and the Buchanan mansion. A *General Hospital* character might work at the hospital itself, live in the Quartermaine mansion or the "brownstone" apartment building, eat at Kelly's Diner (with rooms to rent upstairs), and conduct an illicit affair at the Port Charles Hotel. On NBC's *Another World*, characters live in the Cory mansion or Bayview Court Apartments and work at Cory Publications or the KBAY television station.

These communal work and living spaces result in part from producers' efforts to save money by using a limited number of indoor sets, and they serve scriptwriters' needs by permitting characters to come together easily and logically. The experiences of people who work or live together can be made to overlap plausibly, and if viewers can only be persuaded to accept the idea that adult millionaires with spouses and children would voluntarily continue to live with their parents in the family mansion, such settings can make the most improbable plot complications seem to occur by accident.[15]

Such public spaces are characteristic of all U.S. daytime soap operas, and have a very specific consequence for the way soap characters conduct their lives: They help to create communities in which there is no real division between public and private experience, primarily because much activity and almost all talk takes place in public. Not even places or events whose privacy is considered nearly sacred in the viewers' world are safe from public exposure on the soaps. Bedrooms and doctors' and lawyers' offices are repeatedly invaded, with the result that sexual activities, therapy sessions, and other intimate behaviors are exposed to public view. Yet characters rarely complain about—or even comment on—these intrusions, and in fact seem curiously unaware of the public nature of their surroundings. They make limited efforts to prevent exposure, and the public context of soap opera private life thus becomes naturalized through characters' habit of ignoring and even at times openly denying their lack of privacy.

On *All My Children*, for instance, a psychiatrist experienced two identical intrusions into office therapy sessions in the space of a few months during 1991. In one case, the third side of Erica Kane's latest romantic triangle interrupted a session involving the other two, while in the other, a sexually abusive father broke in at the end of his daughter's session. The routine nature of such violations was underlined by the fact that the doctor and her patients neither asserted the right to confidentiality nor took any precautions to ensure that future sessions would remain private.

Incidents like these intrusions often serve specific dramatic functions in advancing individual storylines—promoting a necessary confrontation between two characters, for example—and so do not necessarily differ significantly from similar events in, say, a conventional prime-time drama. Yet the context in which they occur shifts their meaning considerably. Crucial in determining the entirely public nature of characters' lives—and less immediately tied to specific story developments—is the fact that home, the space that conventionally represents private life, is itself on soaps turned into a public space. The mansions of wealthy families like the Quartermaines, Corys, and Abbotts are perhaps the most extreme examples of this phenomenon, for while other communal or public living arrangements (boarding-houses, shared apartments, hospital quarters) may have practical or economic rationales within their residents' fictional lives, the family home full of wealthy adult characters clearly exists only for the sake of turning the home into a public space.

These group homes do not simply undermine any possibility of private life for individual characters. Paradoxically, the placement of the programs' wealthiest characters in this kind of communal domes-tic situation also overturns their class privilege, suggesting that money cannot buy privacy—or even control over the circumstances of pri-vate life, such as meal selection, decorating decisions, and so on, all of which are represented on soaps as under the control of the (usually male) family head. Such settings also infantalize adult characters by placing them in positions subordinate to the (often tyrannical) fa-ther, permanently trapping them in the role of child, regardless of the power they might yield beyond the family circle.

Yet while the family mansions of the rich may be more typical of the genre as a whole, the *General Hospital* "brownstone" serves as a broader emblem of the communal spaces that dominate soap operas because it is not organized around any version of the traditional nuclear family. The brownstone is a combination boardinghouse/apartment building/family home. The first-floor apartment is occupied by owner and General Hospital nurse Bobbie Spencer Jones, who has shared it with a series of husbands, her adopted children, and an adult step-niece. The rest of the building consists of small self-contained apart-ments occupied by a variety of Bobbie's friends, relatives, hospital coworkers, former lovers, and casual acquaintances. (During 1993, for example, Bobbie shared her own apartment with her husband, General Hospital neurosurgeon Tony Jones, his young daughter, Bobbie's stepdaughter B.J., and their adopted son Lucas; tenants in-cluded their General Hospital coworkers, pediatrician Simone Hardy, her psychiatrist husband Tom, and their baby; Tony and Bobbie's ex-sister-in-law Felicia Jones and her daughter Max; Ryan Chamberlain, a doctor-murderer secretly stalking Felicia; and Bobbie's former lover, lawyer Scott Baldwin.) As landlady, Bobbie frequently invites her tenants in for a meal or drinks, hosts parties, and listens to their problems. She also allows them free entry to her apartment, and they drop in to use her phone, borrow something, or say goodbye on their way in and out of the building.

The absence of privacy inherent in life at the brownstone is exemplified by the problem of Bobbie's door—or rather, her lack of one. Despite a number of building renovations, Bobbie's apartment had until recently no door separating it from the common entryway and staircase. Several years ago, she actually went so far as to order an elaborate set of doors, which for some reason proved impossible to get. Only when an earthquake (yes, in Port Charles, New York) did so much damage that she was required to remodel the entire building did Bobbie finally install, not an apartment door with a lock, but sliding pocket doors, which remain open almost all the time. The brownstone's status as something more like a family home than a boardinghouse or apartment building is underlined by the fact that the only other place on *General Hospital* with large, highly visible interior doors like this is the Quartermaine mansion, where they are used to close off the library, the room in which the family gathers for breakfast, tea, drinks, and acrimonious discussions.

Brownstone residents collude in this view of the building as a unified home, and despite occasional gestures at a separation between their lives, they clearly see themselves as a family. Not only do they walk in and out of each other's apartments, share baby-sitting and other duties, and celebrate holidays and personal landmarks together, they are expected to come to each others' aid in moments of crisis. When Felicia Jones's difficult pregnancy required that she stay in bed for months and her anxious husband Frisco installed a buzzer system, for instance, her neighbors were put on call to rush to her apartment if she needed help. Because most of the residents also have ties through family or work, the fact that they share a home guarantees that their public and private lives will never be separate, and conflicts that originate elsewhere—such as whether to side with Felicia or Ryan in the stalking case—occasionally carry over into domestic life. Indeed, at one time the building actually contained a workplace in the basement, a law office originally used by Bobbie's then-husband Jake and later briefly by tenant Scott Baldwin.

What is most striking about the living arrangements in the brownstone, however, is the extent to which the inhabitants themselves—including Bobbie—deny the building's communal nature. Despite their willingness to behave like a family, they assert their right to privacy, indeed, the *fact* of privacy, sometimes at the very moment of its violation. The epigraph at the beginning of this chapter, in which I quoted Frisco Jones's admission about the impossibility of keeping a secret, represents an unusual acknowledgment of the true situation. Far more typical is Bobbie's insistence, just a month before that, that "we don't intrude on each other's privacy"—spoken immediately after she had intruded on a tenant and her lover in order to extend an invitation to what she called a "welcome-to-the-family" breakfast.[16]

Life in the brownstone demonstrates the extent to which the public context of soap opera private life becomes naturalized through characters' habitual attitudes toward it. Indeed, their behavior goes beyond a simple lack of awareness to gestures of naive faith in their privacy. While the circumstances in which they live and work may, for example, require them to conduct private business in the hospital lounge or brownstone hallway, these circumstances do not require them to confide a secret while standing in front of an open door or window, or over a phone with several extensions. Clearly, soap opera writers are willing to stretch plausibility (including the fact that characters never learn from past mistakes) to provide opportunities for necessary eavesdropping, but once these events occur, even the most transparently contrived occasions acquire meaning within the soaps' construction of privacy, publicity, and community.

The brownstone remains a simultaneously public and private space, but other sites may be defined more fluidly. Lynne Joyrich has remarked on the liminal character of soap opera settings, noting that because the programs express "what are primarily ideological and social conflicts in emotional terms," their action "largely takes place . . . at the intersection[s] of public and private space that are central to personal concerns."[17] But it is crucial to remember that the programs themselves are responsible for defining and constructing many of these public places as personal sites. Soap opera conventions permit a great degree of inconsistency, so that a space that has been established as prime eavesdropping territory—such as a restaurant or lounge—can suddenly be redefined as one in which secrets can be safely exchanged, and vice versa. (Among the most jarring of these redefinitions took place in 1993, when *General Hospital*'s Felicia pretended to be dead in order to trap the murderous Ryan in a plot that involved successfully hiding her in the brownstone attic—despite the fact that Ryan actually lived in the building.) The volume of a conversation or the demeanor of the participants may not give much of a clue to its discreetness; that is, characters often speak at conversational levels regardless of whether they want their words to be audible to others. Instead, the public or private status of a space is often emphasized through camera work and other production techniques. A close-up of two characters speaking together in a General Hospital lounge may suggest that their secret is safe, while in a different scene, a longer shot may reveal not only the public nature of the spot, but even a specific person eavesdropping on them. Far from undermining the programs' conflation of public with private space, however, this mutability emphasizes just how permeable the barrier is between the aspects of life considered private and those that are made public.

The workplaces at the center of U.S. daytime soaps are obviously both chosen and designed to facilitate the blurring of public and private experience. Although her focus on prime-time programs leads her to emphasize a distinction between public and private space that does not apply to daytime serials, Christine Geraghty underlines the way that soaps

> colonise the public sphere and claim it for the personal. . . . Soaps find it virtually impossible to use work settings which deny or suppress the emotional needs of individual characters. . . . Public space also needs to be widely accessible, free-for-all areas where no one can be prevented from joining in a conversation.[18]

This explains, argues Geraghty, the popularity on British serials of settings like Laundromats, stores, and pubs. It also helps us to understand U.S. daytime soaps' use of workplaces that require characters to spend much of their time in public spots like nurses' stations and reception areas.

What Geraghty characterizes as "soaps' strong tendency both to bring personal relationships into the work arena and to deal with relationships at work as if they were [wholly] personal"[19] also helps to explain the programs' preference for setting apparently private expe-

riences in these public locations. This is, of course, closely linked to
soaps' roots in melodrama, which tends, in Christine Gledhill's words,
to understand "the social and political only as they touch on the moral
identities and relationships of individuals."[20] While traditionally private spaces like the home are refigured as public turf through communal living and working arrangements, experiences that viewers
might understand as private—declarations of love, the exchange of
secrets, discussions of intimate family problems—are in turn refigured as public by being set in public locations. Ellen Seiter has described villainesses as particularly prone to public scenes that break
"the rules of social decorum,"[21] but really, nearly every soap opera
character behaves this way at one time or another. While each incident is treated as a unique violation of the distinction between public
and private spheres, the very frequency of such events actually rede-
fines these utterances as commonplace.

A similar process is at work in some of the television programs
that, in Mimi White's view, draw on therapeutic discourse. In shows
like *Divorce Court*, "Viewers are held at a safe distance by the devices
of fictionality even as they hear confessions of an intimate, even potentially sordid, nature."[22] Indeed, although she does not invoke the
parallel directly, many of the traits White detects in certain game and
"reality"-based shows are typical of soaps as well. Like *Divorce Court*,
soap operas "play on the borders of romantic fantasy and middle-
class decorum and propriety" (p. 77), and both kinds of programs
dramatize such fantasy "through a confessional mode of discourse
that itself threatens to transgress the limits of proper middle-class
decorum" (p. 78).[23] White even suggests a potential source of enjoyment for soap opera viewers when she writes that "[t]here is an unde-
niable fascination and pleasure to be derived from witnessing this
overstepping of the bounds of middle-class propriety" (p. 79).[24]

These violations of propriety take place not only through explicit
acts, but also through descriptions of and discussions of those acts,
and through the verbal revelation of emotions conventionally kept
hidden from public view. As many critics and theorists have pointed
out, soap operas are fundamentally dramas of information rather than
action: Much *seems* to happen on them, and characters' lives look like
never-ending cycles of catastrophic events, but compared to self-contained dramas, or even series television, little actually transpires on

any given day of viewing.[25] Whether this is primarily because the serial form requires that information be repeated for viewers who have
missed an episode or because soaps mirror the slow pace of women's
daily domestic lives is for the moment beside the point. Either way,
the fact that they consist mainly of talk lends special significance to
the settings and contexts in which such talk takes place.

It also means that the mere possession of information has a special weight. While characters are positioned within the soap opera
community primarily in terms of kinship networks and romantic relationships, at any given moment each individual's place is also defined
by his or her knowledge. Discovering and controlling access to secret
or private information and the timing of its revelation are therefore
major tools for asserting power and manipulating other characters.
Spying is a time-honored soap opera practice, from the subtle, such
as accidental eavesdropping, to the gross, such as following people,
peeping through windows, or hiring private detectives. All of these
acts are facilitated by the public settings I described earlier, but the
collapse of the distinction between private and public knowledge
through direct inquiry is also a structural feature of the programs.
Characters' constant questioning of each other is a regular aspect of
even the most mundane soap opera dialogue and is, along with setting, a major method of blurring the traditional distinction between
private information and public news.

The soap opera world has its own rules of decorum, of course,
some of which openly contradict the etiquette of the world inhabited
by viewers. Those contradictions help to define the soap opera community and its prerogatives as identifiable fictional entities, and one
of the most prominent among them is characters' freedom to inter-
rogate each other about every detail of their lives. It sometimes seems
as if the questions "where have you been?", "who were you with?",
and "who was that on the phone?" are the most common lines spoken on soap operas. But the fact that such questions are so frequently
asked is less remarkable than the fact that characters thus cross-exam-
ined usually feel obliged to respond. Whether they tell the truth and
thereby reveal information they wanted to keep secret, or lie and
entangle themselves in a complicated skein of deceit, characters almost never simply deny the questioner's right to inquire. They may
offer token resistance, but in the end, they accept it as entirely rea-

sonable for a friend or relative, no matter how distant or estranged, to demand explanations on any subject.

The rare occasions on which characters do refuse to respond to such interrogation actually serve to reinforce community members' right to intrude into others' lives. In the fall of 1991 on *The Young and the Restless*, for example, Nikki Abbott's ex-husband Victor Newman repeatedly demanded that she answer his probing questions about her behavior. Her refusal to do so could have been justified on many grounds, including his long-standing unwillingness to relinquish control of her life, and indeed, she angrily insisted to him that he simply had no business questioning her about her personal life. But viewers knew—and Victor eventually discovered—that the real reason behind her resistance was not an innocent desire for privacy, but something far more sinister: She was desperately trying to hide her drug and alcohol dependence. Thus at the very moment of asserting a right to privacy, the soap opera character acknowledges that only a person with something to hide would really insist on it.

This kind of open conflict over privacy helps to foreground the issue as one of the genre's main concerns. In stories that directly engage the topic, private behavior often erupts dramatically into public discourse, as when a character is forced to reveal the details of a sexual experience in a public setting such as a courtroom, or when such details are made public by a third party. Ironically, however, while the obliteration of individual characters' privacy may structure the programs, the blurring of public and private experience remains the subtext rather than the overt subject of most soap opera stories, and storylines that openly explore the issue's intricacies are actually fairly rare. Occasionally, however, soap operas do make the boundary between public and private concerns their explicit subject. One of the most memorable instances in recent years occurred as a part of *One Life to Live*'s highly publicized 1992 homophobia storyline. While the storyline began by focusing on gay teenager Billy Douglas's dilemma over coming-out to his family and friends, attention quickly shifted to the sexual identity of Llanview minister Andrew Carpenter.[26] Although Andrew was clearly marked on the program as heterosexual (via his earlier unrequited love for one woman and his ongoing sexual and romantic involvement with another), a troubled young woman whose advances he had rejected spread a rumor that he was homosexual, igniting a scandal over Andrew's fitness as both a minister and a youth counselor. While he could have stopped the scandal at any moment by simply declaring his heterosexuality, as his close friends and family urged him to do, Andrew refused to answer questions about his sexual identity on the grounds that his sexual behavior was an entirely private matter that had no bearing on his public position within the Llanview or church communities. Despite being socially and professionally ostracized, alienated from his girl-friend, locked out of his church, and subjected to a violent physical attack, and regardless of the arguments of those closest to him, Andrew refused to discuss his sexuality, insisting to the bitter end that his privacy be respected. And he eventually convinced enough prominent church and town figures of the rightness of his stance to save his job and position.

Andrew's struggle to maintain his privacy was presented within the program as an honorable pursuit, supported, albeit reluctantly, by those *One Life to Live* characters usually associated with goodness and morality, notably Viki Lord Buchanan. Those characters who opposed him were depicted, not simply as unsympathetic or conservative, but as bigoted, homophobic, and closed-minded, linked with vicious verbal slurs and violent assaults on those they suspected of being gay. The outcome of the storyline fully vindicated Andrew's position, but paradoxically, in fighting for his right to an entirely private sexual identity, he violated a basic imperative of soap opera community life: the necessity of permitting others to intrude in one's life.

It is crucial to understand that the right to intrude on what viewers might perceive as others' private business is based, not on expertise, but on simple membership in the soap opera community. Community membership grants all characters an equal stake in the lives of their relatives and neighbors. It follows that if nearly anyone is allowed to ask questions about nearly anything, most people also feel free to dispense unasked-for advice to others. Qualifications such as success in a similar area of personal relations are unnecessary, and even characters who have, say, a long trail of failed unions behind them blithely advise others on how to maintain their marriages, while parents who have spent years in conflict with their children suggest ways to strengthen family ties.

This conviction about the universal right to know and advise engenders chains of invasive behavior, some as ludicrous as the one that occurred toward the end of the 1991 *Young and the Restless* storyline about Nikki's substance abuse. During that story, Nikki's husband Jack Abbott was in a perpetual state of rage over Victor's interference in their lives, yet almost the moment Nikki's crisis ended, Jack eagerly began to perform the same operation on his father John. At one point, for instance, he strolled casually into John's bedroom and, finding him in bed with a woman Jack detests, insisted that John heed his, Jack's, advice and dump her. Although his father eventually asked Jack to leave, John's nearly expressionless reaction testified eloquently to his acceptance of this bit of soap opera protocol.

Jack Abbott's behavior is classic. He is notorious for intervening in his father's life, and he offers the typical soap opera justification: concern for the well-being of others. A January 1993 exchange with Mamie, the Abbott family housekeeper, is a typical expression of his conviction that interference equals caring:

> Mamie: I will not spy on your father in his own house.
> Jack: Don't think of it as spying—think of it as protecting him.
> . . . Do it for Dad's sake.

The result of such insistent intrusions, of course, is to make the most intimate aspects of characters' lives the subject of public knowledge and discussion. Where manipulative characters like Jack Abbott or Victor Newman are concerned, there may be other, more far-reaching results as well, namely, the loss of control over private choices and personal decisions.

Soap opera's constant exposure of private, even secret, information is in part a function of the genre's relationship to traditional melodrama, a relationship that I have already argued is problematic. Still, like stage and film melodramas—in which, as Peter Brooks writes, "Nothing is spared because nothing is left unsaid"[27]—soaps exteriorize emotion by permitting viewers to see into characters' hearts and minds through techniques like the spoken interior monologue.[28] In Lynne Joyrich's words, "psychological conflicts are externalized so that they may be clear as fundamental forces. It is in the clash and play of their visible oppositions that melodrama's meaning becomes both legible and consumable."[29]

Central to this entire process is the fact that soap opera viewers are nearly always in a position of knowledge superior to any individual character.[30] While they are not granted absolute omniscience, viewers possess most of the narrative's secrets, and inevitably know more than the characters themselves, from whom important pieces of information are often concealed as crucial parts of the ongoing stories.[31] Tania Modleski and others have argued that this near-omniscience contributes to viewers' capacity to identify with a number of different characters, offering multiple simultaneous opportunities for identification in place of the one-to-one relationship typical of more conventional film and TV narratives.[32] In the context of the soaps' treatment of privacy, however, it also functions to make every character's most private experiences and feelings public, turning the viewer into a kind of voyeur.

Still, as I have already made clear, soap operas simultaneously expose each character's inner feelings and thoughts to other characters just as clearly as they are exteriorized for viewers. This is in some ways the *subject* of soap opera, and there are a number of reasons why this constant violation of characters' privacy should continue to play a central role in soap opera narrative. John Hartley has called the programs' obsession with talk a mark of soap opera communities' status as "symbolic paedocracies" that are "de-centered into adolescence," full of

> endless talk of self-discovery and personal relationships. . . . Everyone is easily distracted from occupational tasks in order to talk, and whilst talk of *public* affairs and politics is rare and embarrassing, there's little sense of individual or even family *privacy*, either.[33]

Hartley's pejorative language, however, nearly obscures a useful insight into soap talk's role in opening all areas of personal life to public scrutiny, and the importance of the exchange of information—the passing on of secrets and confidences—not only to the forward motion of the soap opera storyline, but to the construction of the soap opera community itself.

A helpful approach may come from Gloria-Jean Masciarotte's analysis of the discourse of daytime talk shows, which she discusses in terms that seem equally appropriate for soap operas. Talk shows, she writes, "constitute emphatically a movement away from private citizen to social citizen," their narrative dependent on "the spectacle of talk."[34] Like the programs Masciarotte describes, soap operas also operate through the passing on of gossip and the exchange of stories, and—like *The Oprah Winfrey Show* in particular—threaten to erase "the important bourgeois distinction of private and public" (p. 94).

Following Masciarotte's analysis—particularly her suspicion that talk shows are denigrated precisely because they exhibit women's unruly talk about "the painful experiences or the uncured activity" (p. 104n.)—we might consider daytime talk shows and soap operas as nonfictional and fictional versions of the same "endless narrative of discomfort" (p. 83), sharing as well a broad cultural label as "trash" aimed at bored women viewers.

However, while it is true that soap opera communities make secrecy impossible and require characters to submit their experiences to constant public scrutiny, the programs also replicate nostalgic fantasies about the intimacy of the traditional family or small town. Once again, this may be a heritage of the medium's early days when, as Lynn Spigel argues, the "nightmarish vision of the preplanned [suburban] community served as an impetus for the arrival of a surrogate community on television. Television provided an illusion of the ideal neighborhood—the way it was supposed to be."[35] In fact, claims Spigel, early television's invocation of community was more complex than the simple replacement of an inadequate real-life experience with a friendlier TV version: "It promised modes of spectator pleasure premised upon the sense of an illusory—rather than a real—community of friends," while at the same time placing "the ideals of community togetherness . . . *at a fictional distance*," thus relieving viewers of the potential guilt of isolating themselves within their homes.[36]

Such distancing continues in today's soap operas, and on it depends a degree of the enjoyment viewers experience. Writing of the British serial *EastEnders*, David Buckingham suggests that television allows viewers "to look without being seen, . . . to pass comment without fear of reprisals."[37] In fact, he contends that habitual viewers maintain a degree of critical distance from the programs they watch, enabling a "questioning and even ridiculing [of] the artificiality of the programme."[38] (Such an activity is only possible, of course, among viewers who are fully aware that they are watching a fictional show. Despite the popular stereotype of the soap opera fan's inability to tell fact from fantasy, research demonstrates that viewers know perfectly well that they are watching a fictional program.)

But the pleasure viewers gain by watching soaps surely extends beyond the merely voyeuristic. Soap opera villainesses and busybodies may feel free to intrude into every aspect of their neighbors' lives, but other characters feel equally welcome to express their sincere concern and to come to their friends' aid. If we think back, not only to Spigel's depiction of early TV, but to the genre's specific origins in radio and then again in the early years of television as entertainment for women working in their homes, their days supposedly focused on family and other domestic concerns, it is easy to imagine the attraction of a fictional community in which no one is ever truly isolated and no one has to confront difficult family problems alone. Jane Feuer has claimed that "the main fantasy of the soap opera remains that of a fully self-sufficient family,"[39] but I see the genre's insistence that all community members have an intimate stake in each other's lives as instead privileging the caring community over the family—and even promoting it, in some cases, as a source of refuge from and support in dealing with a family that is, according to the logic of the soap opera narrative, in perpetual crisis.

Patricia Meyer Spacks's study of gossip suggests another possible source of women's pleasure in soap opera's collapse of the private into the public, one that has particular relevance to the televisual exposure to viewers of characters' lives. Spacks writes that "journalistic gossip" like that practiced by *People* magazine and the tabloid press "declares the universal comprehensibility of other people's lives,"[40] and she describes the commercial purveyors of gossip as "claim[ing] for the public realm material traditionally belonging to the private. Such eliding of boundaries reveals an upswell of acknowledged interest in private matters at the same time that it effectively denies the notion of privacy" (p. 259). I think it can be argued that soap operas do the same, although they do it through admitted fiction. The constant revelation of the most intimate details of personal life offers viewers the opportunity to understand fully the motivations, emotions, familial, romantic, and sexual experiences, and even the criminal activities of characters who are, after 2 or 10 or 20 years of viewing, as familiar as our own friends and relatives. Because characters' lives are thus made to seem transparent, while those of one's real family and acquaintances remain obstinately opaque, soaps offer what Lynne Joyrich has characterized as "[m]elodrama's promise of universally legible meaning."[41]

Yet the two sides of this elision of public and private life are inextricably entwined, and soap operas' view of the individual's relation to her or his community is a paradoxical one. As Christine Geraghty notes, "The very transparency of life within the community, their openness to each other, makes individual members vulnerable."[42] David Buckingham makes a similar point in his book about the British serial *EastEnders*: "The need for community support . . . [is] in conflict with the need for privacy which is so vital for many of the characters, if their secrets are to be kept hidden."[43] It has become a critical truism to say that soap operas invest even the most private events with public significance, that they refigure traditionally domestic questions of love and family as of compelling interest to everyone. But the communal nature of soap opera experience goes farther than that, erasing the traditional boundary between private and public life and helping to engender a community in which no secrets are possible because all of life takes place in public.

In this optimistic mood, it is tempting to go a step further, and to see the soaps' virtual destruction of the private realm as a protofeminist, if not in fact a consciously feminist gesture. If we understand the domestic/private sphere as a primary site of women's oppression, we might then try to understand soaps as undermining the entire notion of "separate spheres" by drawing traditionally private issues into public. I want to caution, however, against this interpretation for a very specific reason. Although I have been arguing that the programs effectively destroy the very notion of privacy by redefining conventionally private sites and concerns as public, it is crucial to point out that in doing so, soap operas also strip them of whatever political or social meaning they might have.

This depoliticization is not, however, unique to soap opera, but is of a piece with the rest of patriarchal ideology, including the other cultural and social operations and institutions that encourage us, as I pointed out at the beginning of this chapter, to see a rigid separation between supposedly apolitical "private" life and a "public" sphere that is the proper site of political and social activity. Soap operas thus demonstrate what Thomas Elsaesser has identified as commercial popular culture's habit of "resolutely refus[ing] to understand social change in other than private contexts and emotional terms,"[44] while simultaneously maintaining the dominant definition of those "private contexts" as beyond the reach of politics. This is the other side of the "publicity" that attends soap characters' private experiences: There are no politics—and there is therefore no feminism—in the soap opera community. In the following two chapters we will see some of the ideological consequences of that fact.

4

How Things End: The Problem of Closure

> How things end can throw previous experi-
> ence into unexpected perspective.
>
> —Laura Mulvey, "Melodrama Inside and
> Outside the Home"

■ Despite the wide variety of perspectives from which critics and theorists approach soap opera, there is one point of agree-
ment, and it has come to shape an understanding of the entire genre:
the contention that soap operas are uniquely marked by a lack of
narrative closure. Typical are Robert Allen's assertion that a "central
aesthetic characteristic of the soap opera is its absolute resistance to
narrative closure"[1] and Dennis Porter's statement that the soap's "purpose clearly is to never end."[2] Jerry Palmer goes so far as to argue that
"[i]n the instance of soap opera there is no such thing as a text . . .
since the stories in question have no end."[3] In fact, the idea that
soaps do not offer narrative closure has become so widely accepted
that Susan Willis can refer to it in a discussion of commodity packag-
ing as something that "we all know."[4]

Other theorists step back a bit from the extremity of this claim.
Christine Geraghty, for example, talks about the impossibility of "clos-
ing" a soap opera, but describes the genre as offering "temporary
resolution,"[5] while Sandy Flitterman-Lewis argues that the programs
provide "pseudo-endings," partial resolutions "which inevitably per-

mit the further elaboration of the text."[6] Jeremy Butler claims that soap operas focus on the "diegetic middle: enigmas without permanent resolutions,"[7] while Lynne Joyrich writes that their lack of resolution means that "soap operas ultimately reject the notion of progress," trapping both viewers and characters "in an eternally conflictual present."[8]

This presumed lack of closure is seen not simply as a defining characteristic of the soap opera narrative, but as a major source of women's pleasure in the genre, and it figures prominently in assessments of the programs' ideological function. Such critical unanimity, however, obscures the important ways in which soap operas *do* offer opportunities for closure and it therefore actually limits our ability to understand how the genre operates ideologically. In this chapter, I want to consider the many ways closure works across the soap opera narrative, and what its appearance implies both for soap opera theory and for broader questions in television studies.

Let me begin with an example that demonstrates how soap opera theorists have dealt with the issue of closure. In "All's Well That Doesn't End," Sandy Flitterman-Lewis insists that weddings, usually seen as emblems of closure in classical cinema and traditional drama, have an initiating rather than a resolving function in soap operas. She sees the soap opera convention of the interrupted wedding as an eruption of cinematic "memory" into the televisual organization of the soap, and uses the examples of two *General Hospital* weddings—each disrupted by the sudden recollection of a past traumatic incident—to demonstrate that such events provide only "pseudo-endings" rather than full or permanent resolutions.

Her argument that soap opera weddings do not serve their traditional dramatic purpose is a compelling one, but her examples actually offer evidence that soap operas provide closure precisely at the level of the individual storyline. The key is in how we describe the parameters of that storyline. If we shift our attention away from cinematic expectations and realign Flitterman-Lewis's plots, for instance—orienting them not around the weddings she describes, but around the memories that disrupt them—we can see that both Camilia's and Terry's successful recollections provide resolutions to storylines that preexist the weddings themselves. They represent, in fact, the *conclusions* of storylines organized around specific mysteries that can be summarized as searches for the traumas these women experienced.

Discussions of soap opera closure have tended to focus on the serial nature of the programs, and that concentration has, I believe, led critics to behave as if the irresolution that characterizes the soap opera as a *serial* necessarily operates across every aspect of its narrative. In what follows, I will argue that soap opera storylines are capable, not simply of "temporary" or "partial" resolution, but of as complete a closure as is possible on any continuing television series. Because soap operas are marked by overlapping and intertwined plots, their complex entanglement can sometimes make it difficult to separate the resolution of one storyline from the development of another, but many—perhaps most—storylines are resolved in some way. And while such closure may lay the groundwork for a later reopening, such "reopening" is precisely that: the opening of something previously closed, not the continuation of something that never closed to begin with.

This distinction will be clearer if we first consider four levels at which closure could potentially occur. The greatest in scale is the televisual level, the program itself. *General Hospital*, for instance, is first of all the specific ABC daytime drama that began production in 1963 and currently airs for an hour each day, five days a week. As a television show, *General Hospital* will not achieve full "closure" of any sort until it is canceled.

I should note here that there is some question about whether cancellation would actually constitute closure. Jerry Palmer, for instance, writes that "even when a given soap ceases broadcasting, the stories are not ended, in the usual sense, for it is impossible to resolve so many plot lines—they simply cease being told."[9] In fact, the recent final episodes of soaps like *Generations* (1991) and *Santa Barbara* (1993) have tended to tie up some storylines while leaving others open, but Henry Jenkins's work on TV fandom makes it clear that, regardless of any finale's efforts to unravel the narrative enigmas of a series, some viewers refuse to accept the end of the broadcast or cable run as the end of the story.[10] However, while the end of a series does not necessarily answer every question—or satisfy all viewers—it nevertheless represents a particular form of closure: the end of storytelling, the moment (barring movie sequels) beyond which no more will be revealed.

At the diegetic level, *General Hospital* consists of, but is not identical to, the fictional events concerning the eponymous General Hospital and the city of Port Charles, its residents, and their densely intertwined lives. Because both the hospital and the larger community have ongoing fictional existences that coincide with the history of the program, this level, too, offers no hope of closure—short of a disaster that erases the city and its inhabitants from the globe. Although these "fictional existences" are expressed through specific storylines, they actually consist, not of the stories themselves, but of a web of family, romantic, political, criminal, professional, and other relationships among the show's characters, the material out of which the stories are made. This is the arena in which what Christine Geraghty has described as the "overall hermeneutic" of the traditional soap is carried out—"the long-term changes in feelings and characters."[11] It is important to retain that idea as we consider exactly what constitutes the soap opera narrative, and therefore what might constitute its end. For the moment, an example will suffice: The *relationship* between former spouses Lucy Coe and Alan Quartermaine has a long history and is likely to continue in some form as long as both remain among the show's characters, but few *stories* actually bring the two characters together in any significant way. While they frequently spend on-screen time together, often referring to their shared past, those moments rarely advance any storyline's narrative development. Barring one or the other's departure from the program, the relationship between Lucy and Alan has no potential for closure, although any individual stories in which they become involved may be resolved in a variety of ways.

At the other end of the televisual scale is the episode, also typically characterized by irresolution. Here, nonclosure may be directly expressed through dramatic cliff-hanger endings, but it is usually signaled in far less explicit ways. Rather than being tied up within a single episode, as they would be in traditional series television, problems and questions continue to build across several days, weeks, and months. This is not to say, however, that "in all cases narrative questions are left open" at an episode's conclusion, as Verina Glaessner has claimed.[12] In fact, the end of an episode does occasionally coincide with the resolution of specific events. Even more often, an episode ends with the provision of an important piece of information that provides a kind of miniclosure very similar to the conclusions of conventional television episodes. The final scene may, for instance, depict a long-deferred reunion, a romantic consummation, or the revelation of a character's identity. (Thus, to choose just one example, on August 31, 1990, *General Hospital* ended by clearly establishing a particular character as a murderer. In the penultimate scene, a journalist seeking the as-yet-unidentified murderer claimed to have just missed catching him, and the final shot of the episode—which immediately followed this statement—consisted of the killer turning to face the camera.) Nevertheless, soap operas represent a paradigmatic example of the serial form, and it is the overall tendency to episodic nonresolution that distinguishes a serial from a conventional episodic series.

Yet somewhere between that single episode and the whole that is *General Hospital* lies the individual storyline, and it is at this in-between point that closure can and does take place. Experienced viewers find it relatively simple to follow the trajectory of a specific storyline, even when it is entangled with several others, and this sorting out of storylines is probably a source of considerable enjoyment for them.[13] Even more important, I want to argue that regular viewers expect and anticipate resolution—indeed watch for it, predict when and how it will occur, and speculate on its implications and consequences for other characters and storylines.

Even critics who insist that soap operas themselves provide no real closure acknowledge that such a lack may be frustrating for viewers accustomed to the end-orientation of conventional narratives. Sandy Flitterman-Lewis, for instance, makes the intriguing argument that *commercials* satisfy soap viewers' desire for the closure she believes is missing from the programs themselves: "Far from interrupting the narrative flow of stimulated yearning for a just conclusion and perpetual indication of its impossibility, commercials are small oases of narrative closure."[14]

I believe that this longing for closure plays an important part in the soap opera viewing experience. But I want to go beyond the possibility that viewers are so intent on seeking closure in the programs they watch that they impose their own desires for resolution onto narratives that actually refuse such tidy ends. Instead, I want to argue that, far from being marked by a unique lack of closure, soaps are actually characterized by just the opposite: an excess of resolving gestures. Paradoxically, it may be this very profusion that has encouraged critics to see soaps as totally lacking in traditional narrative resolution.

Before we consider exactly how closure occurs and what it might mean, however, we need to define it more specifically. One thing that rapidly becomes clear is that definitions based on traditional written narratives cannot easily be applied to the soap opera text. In his work on closure in the novel, for instance, D. A. Miller has identified the "narratable" as "the instances of disequilibrium, suspense, and general insufficiency from which a given narrative appears to arise."[15] Although he treats closure as an essentially artificial intervention meant to end an otherwise interminable narrative, he argues that closure is basically the opposite of narratability—is, in other words, the point at which no more can be said within narrative. If Miller is correct, then no closure of any sort is ever possible within soap opera, for it is impossible to imagine a moment when all that can be said has been said. This is a central feature of the soap opera as serial and of its narrative strategies in general. To ensure the continuing drama, the long-running serial must exist in a perpetual state of actual and potential "disequilibrium," full of the as-yet-unexpressed possibilities of future stories. (Despite Miller's contention, in fact, this is to some extent true of all narratives, since even the most complete kind of closure inevitably leaves some excess of narratable material.)[16]

But such potentiality is not simply a function of the serial form's insatiable appetite for conflict. It arises directly from soap opera's obsession with private life, especially its interest in individual feelings and in the emotional consequences of behavior. As I argued in chapter 3, within the close-knit soap opera community, there is no such thing as an event that can incite no further response in anyone, or a problem about which no more can be spoken. Although scriptwriters rarely feel compelled to explore all the possible reverberations, soaps depend on the fact that every relationship, every family, every person, every occurrence is capable of arousing infinite interest, is open to endless debate, analysis, reinterpretation, and speculation. There is always someone whose reaction has not yet been heard, someone whose life has not yet been fully considered in light of the latest development. And unlike the traditional novels of Miller's study, soap operas contain no genuinely—or at least no irreversibly—peripheral figures. Every character, however minor, can become engaged in a crisis, and every event, however trivial or apparently straightforward, can become a serious conundrum. After all, as Robert Allen points out, "The soap opera makes the consequences of actions more important than action itself."[17]

I raise the subject of these complex community ties here primarily to suggest the extent to which the intertwined storylines of a soap opera differ from the more linear design of a conventional novel. A definition like Miller's is designed to explain closure in a traditional written narrative that follows the trajectory of a single plot, and this is clearly inappropriate for the continuing multiple dramas of soap opera. But even more important, theories of closure based on published novels, in which the end of the story exists before we read its beginning, may not be applicable to the television production process, where the end of a series is by no means implicit—or even existent—at its beginning. Not only is the ending of a particular storyline or program often undecided when production begins, but it may change suddenly after being written or even filmed. (Consider the case of CBS's *Magnum, p.i.*, which ended production with a 1987 "finale" in which its protagonist actually died—only to be resurrected when star Tom Selleck agreed to continue the series for another season.) Because of their production schedule—programs are usually taped only two weeks in advance of broadcast—and producers' eagerness both to incorporate the real-world calendar and to be responsive to viewers, soap operas are simply the most extreme demonstration of what is actually a major feature of all television production. Across (U.S. commercial) television, stories, characters, casting, even furniture and costume details may be altered in direct response to ratings, viewer or sponsor complaints, political or cultural events beyond the program, and so on.

This capacity for extratextually motivated, after-the-fact alterations marks a major difference between TV and traditional print fictions, whose content, once committed to paper, is necessarily fixed to a far greater degree than a program that has not yet been aired. Although soap operas may make greater use of it than other fictional programming, the almost infinite erasability of events is a component of the "liveness" that attaches to every telecast, regardless of the actual relationship between the occurrence of an event and its TV transmission.[18] This in turn means that the notion of TV "narratability" must be rethought, for even an event whose dramatic consequences seem to have been exhausted—an event about which it appears no more can be said—can be easily revived. Instead of positing television closure as the absolute end of narratability, then, and therefore concluding that no such end can occur in soap opera, we need to consider what sort of closure *is* possible.

One of the difficulties in establishing this, however, involves the vexing problem of defining and identifying the soap opera plot. Yet the very word "plot" raises special problems, not least because it immediately suggests the related term "subplot"—a concept that is entirely meaningless within the context of soap opera narrative. In a sense, all stories within a soap opera are "subplots" of the overarching fiction of the program, for an outline of any single soap's complex tangle of stories demonstrates nothing so much as the absolute contingency of every event within it.[19] Can there be, after all, any such thing as a genuinely *noncontingent* event in a drama that deals with a closed group of characters intimately related to each other by ties of blood, romance, work, and history?

As if this were not enough, there is the additional fact that formula-driven narratives like soap operas rework the same basic elements over and over again, often involving the same group of characters in identical settings. In some ways, the closed community of an individual soap opera resembles book series like those centered on James Bond or V. I. Warshawski, in which an essential problematic—the Cold War, the battle against Chicago crime—is repeated from story to story. While we need to keep in mind at all times the difficulty of transferring to television theoretical concepts developed to explain novels and other print narratives, it seems reasonable to turn to such works of formula fiction to find a way of talking about how soap opera narratives function.

In their work on James Bond, Tony Bennett and Janet Woollacott have usefully distinguished between *plot*—"the regular and repeatable elements which recur across the Bond novels"—and *story*—"the way in which, in a particular novel, such elements are organised into a temporally and causally coherent sequence."[20] Since each soap opera consists of a dozen or more storylines, the analogy is not really between an individual program and a particular novel, but between an individual storyline and a single novel, and between a program— say, *General Hospital*—and the Bond or Warshawski novels as a group. The entire collection of commercial U.S. daytime soaps would thus perhaps be analogous to the genre of the spy thriller or the feminist mystery.[21]

Just as each series in the mystery or thriller genre idiosyncratically reworks a similar set of themes and motifs—Sue Grafton does not write exactly the same novels as Sara Paretsky, yet they make use of the same basic material—so the programs that comprise the soap opera genre repeatedly raise the same questions about family and romance. As with any formula fiction, the genre's presentation of these issues has become highly codified, organized into particular formulations and conventions, dependent on similar narrative and dramatic strategies (such as coincidence, chains of secrecy and revelation, and so on). Thus, while each series presents its own individual set of characters and situations, specific storylines essentially provide often predictable variations on highly familiar plots (such as the paternity mystery or tales of thwarted love) involving stock types of characters (the villainess, the good mother, the evil seducer).[22]

While I do not intend to argue that every enigma posed within a program will necessarily be developed into a full-blown story, let me propose a simple definition of a soap opera storyline as a narrative that traces the temporal trajectory of a specific question or enigma and can be described in terms of it (will these characters marry? who killed that person? and so on). Following Bennett and Woollacott, I then reserve the term "plot" for those underlying elements that recur across the soap opera genre, such as the mysteries of paternal identity that I will analyze in chapter 5. I don't mean to suggest that some rigid set of myths or rules underlies the soap opera narrative, but that the genre is interested in a particular set of issues that revolve around the family, romance, sexuality, community, and women's identity. Because the programs share this common interest, are produced within the same commercial television structure, and target the same basic audience, they tend to present very similar versions of their underlying story elements. All current commercial U.S. soaps explore questions about love, loyalty, kinship, friendship, and community as those issues are traditionally inflected by gender. *General Hospital* works through them in the particular context of Port Charles and its hospital and through the experiences of a specific set of characters, while CBS's *The Young and the Restless* does the same with its own characters in Genoa City.

My definition of closure is equally simple: It occurs when the basic question that propelled a story is answered or when its central enigma is explained.[23] (Enigmas that are maintained below the level of a fully developed storyline are also likely to be resolved, but answers to their motivating questions do not constitute closure in the same sense.) Although it arises logically and causally from the content of a specific storyline, closure is at base an artificial narrative strategy rather than some "natural" or inevitable conclusion. The ending of any given story could in principle be deferred indefinitely, nor is any particular resolution inevitable. However, because soap operas adhere closely to a set of story formulas, many conclusions are highly predictable, which often makes them *seem* like the only way events could have turned out. And like all endings, the achievement of closure lends a retrospective air of inevitability to a story's development. In Barthes's words, "Writing 'the end' . . . thus posits everything that has been written as having been a tension which 'naturally' requires resolution."[24]

While conventional distinctions like plot and subplot may be inadequate to describe soap opera complications, however, we do need to be able to talk both about those clusters of stories that are closely connected to each other and about what we might provisionally describe as the relative autonomy among those clusters. For this purpose, I adopt the term *arc*, which has in recent years been used to describe the narratives of prime-time series that combine the conventions of episodic and serial television (such as CBS's *Wiseguy*),[25] although the concept necessarily needs to be reworked somewhat to describe soap opera narratives. On episodic programs, an arc is a storyline that extends beyond a single episode but does not express the basic problematic of the series, and arcs are usually resolved after several episodes. (On *Wiseguy*, for instance, the series' central problematic centered on Vinnie Terranova's ongoing work as an undercover federal agent, while multi-episode arcs concerned his infiltration of individual organized crime families.) The use of story arcs thus brings to certain programs the serial convention of episodic nonresolution without turning them into serials, much less into soap operas.[26]

In discussing soap operas, however, I want to use the notion of the arc in a slightly different way in order to make it easier to discuss the connections among specific stories and groups of stories. On soaps and other serials, I am defining an arc as a group of related storylines and narrative enigmas that are linked dramatically—because they involve the same group of characters and often the same events—as well as temporally, and whose developments are immediately or directly dependent on each other to a greater degree than the loosely contingent relationships among characters and events across the program. The arc thus represents a narrative level *between* the individual storyline and the larger fictional web of community relationships, and like those ongoing ties, arcs do not easily reach closure. Instead, as old storylines are resolved, new ones tend to be incorporated into an existing arc so that its content changes gradually over time.

For example, *One Life to Live*'s highly publicized homophobia story, which developed during the summer of 1992, was actually the main focus of an arc consisting of several related and closely entangled storylines and enigmas, not all of them about homophobia. Among them were the stories of minister Andrew Carpenter's romance with Cassie; his confrontation with the church hierarchy and the town of Llanview over his own behavior and sexuality; Andrew's struggle to reconcile his father, Sloan, to Andrew's brother's homosexuality and death from AIDS; Marty's plot to punish Andrew for rejecting her sexual advances; Billy Douglas's coming-out story; Joey and Alana's romance and their friendship with Billy; Clint and Viki Buchanan's increasing estrangement; Viki's growing friendship with Sloan; and the progress of Sloan's illness.[27] While these individual *stories* were each capable of reaching resolutions of various kinds, the arc itself continued far beyond them, shifting its focus—from, for example, the crisis over Billy's homosexuality to the tensions in Andrew and Cassie's romance to the collapse of Viki and Clint's marriage—as component stories were resolved.

To a certain extent, the arc can be described in terms of the *relationships* directly involved in it: Viki and Clint's relationships with each other and with their sons, Kevin and Joey; Viki's with Andrew,

Sloan, the Douglases, and the other members of the church; Andrew's with Sloan, Cassie, Marty, Billy, and the church hierarchy; Billy's with Marty, Joey, Alana, and his parents; Cassie's with her mother Dorian; and Joey's with Alana. This cluster of relationships in turn takes place within the larger community of Llanview, where these and other characters are tied together through a complex range of kinship and other bonds, but do not necessarily all become involved in overlapping storylines. (Dorian and Kevin, for instance, while closely related to several of the main participants in this arc, had only tangential roles in it, while other major characters, such as Asa Buchanan, had no real place at all.) And it is crucial to remember that, although the homophobia-related stories and the larger Andrew-Billy-Viki-centered arc that encompassed them occupied a lot of character, viewer, and press attention, other major arcs moved forward at the same time, including the ones centering on (but not fully defined by) Tina and Cain's plan to entrap Alex; the romantic entanglements of Luna, Max, Blair, and Suede; and Lee Ann, Kevin, and Jason's divorce/custody/ kidnapping story.

As my earlier comments on Flitterman-Lewis's analysis of *General Hospital* demonstrate, whether and how fully we understand a particular storyline to be resolved obviously depends to a considerable degree on how and where we draw the boundary between it and all the other stories on the program, what specific events we include in one and exclude from another. This is complicated by the fact that, by definition, events within a particular arc usually have important implications for several different storylines. In the *One Life to Live* arc, for example, Andrew's campaign against homophobia offered a point of overlap among at least three narrative threads: Billy Douglas's coming-out, the confrontation over Andrew's own sexuality and behavior as a minister, and Sloan's denial of his other son William's homosexuality. The story centering on Andrew's personal life ended when he successfully reunited the fractured town and congregation by bringing the Names Project AIDS Quilt to Llanview—an event that also led directly to closure of the storyline concerning Sloan's denials about William and brought the main part of Billy's coming-out story to an end.

The larger arc, however, continued to track the implications of earlier developments. Billy's reconciliation with his mother did not

exhaust the consequences of his coming-out, a fact that was emphasized by his classmates' subsequent homophobic attacks and his father's
ongoing hostility. But the story of Andrew and Cassie's romance
immediately became far more prominent than it had been, taking the
place of the homophobia-centered storylines as the arc's major focus.
And by November, the arc had been largely transformed, with Viki
and Clint's marriage and her attraction to Sloan having become its
main concern.[28] What held these stories together as an arc throughout these shifts in emphasis, however, was their continuing temporal
and dramatic entanglement: the fact that the same group of characters remained involved with each other, that events in one story im-
pinged directly on the course of others, and that later storylines continued to explore the ramifications of the arc's earlier stories.[29]

This multiplicity has some very specific significance for soap operas' narrative strategies. A single soap may have as many as 12 or 15
concurrent fully developed storylines or major narrative enigmas—
perhaps three to five arcs—yet a single soap opera episode typically
advances only three or four stories. This means that viewers and characters are always in danger of being overwhelmed by an excess of
plotting. Without some way of moving out of individual stories, so
much diegetic time would eventually be taken up with existent stories that nothing new could happen. Obviously, this echoes Miller's
insistence that closure provides an artificial end to an otherwise un-
ending narrative, but the stakes are somewhat different here, for the
existence of multiple ongoing arcs ensures the continuing presence
of a stable group of characters and allows the programs to explore the
long-term consequences of specific events. Still, closure of some sort
is needed, not to cut off the further implications of specific events,
but to permit viewers and characters to devote time to other stories.
Closure's purpose in soap opera, then, is not to mark the end of
narratability, but the end of *narration*—to allow characters to go on
to new stories and problems and thus to allow the ongoing narrative
to continue.

Let us now return to the possible opportunities for closure within
the soap opera narrative. As I have already suggested, soap opera
closure takes several different forms. There are, to begin with, instances of resolutions as total as those of any traditional novel: the

absolute, on-screen identification of a dead body, for example, or a definitive genetic test establishing paternity. Although on-screen death can bring any sort of story to a definite end, *full closure* is especially common in stories such as murder or paternity mysteries, where the discovery of one incontrovertible fact can answer the question that has powered the narrative. Such resolutions completely end their storylines—and on rare occasions, an entire story arc— although the achievement of closure may itself generate new stories. But these are not the only kinds of stories that achieve full closure. Storylines whose main enigma is, for instance, whether or not a particular couple will fall in love or get married can obviously be resolved when the event occurs. Similar complete resolutions are possible for enigmas that have not been developed into full storylines, such as *One Life to Live*'s question, "Will Andrew persuade Sloan to accept William's homosexuality?", which was definitively answered.

I do not mean to underestimate the complexity of these stories' entanglement with other parts of the program's narrative. The fact that an event which resolves one story often initiates another helps, I think, to obscure the frequency with which stories actually do reach closure, and the very existence of ongoing story arcs obscures it even further. Even greater confusion may arise from the fact that full closure often serves extratextual as much as—occasionally even more than—narrative ends. As Ellen Seiter has pointed out, and as is clear from even the most casual survey of soap fan magazines, "When an actor leaves the show or when a particular storyline is phased out due to adverse audience reaction, narratives are quickly resolved."[30]

Yet to say that the frequency of closure is obscured is not the same as saying that it cannot be discerned—and far less that it does not take place. In fact, soap operas feature several kinds of closure, among which I want to distinguish traditional full closure from strategies that I call *snares, equivocations, temporary closure,* and *series-style* closure. The first two terms are examples of the delays that Barthes identifies as a necessary part of the hermeneutic code, features that arrest an enigma's rush toward full closure,[31] while the other two represent adaptations of traditional narrative closure to suit the soap opera form. An individual storyline has the potential to reach almost any kind of resolution, but the actual type achieved has different consequences for the development of future storylines.[32]

Although Barthes defines the term somewhat more generally, I want to identify a hermeneutic *snare* as a kind of false closure, an apparent resolution that depends directly on a lie, misrepresentation, or misunderstanding. (For example, a body may be accidentally misidentified or one character may deliberately mislead another.) In fact, the audience is sometimes not completely "snared" or misled, precisely because it knows something that is hidden from characters or that directly contradicts their beliefs. It is not necessary for viewers to recognize the falsity of the resolution, but when this kind of disjunction does occur, *characters* continue their lives as if a particular problem has been resolved, while *viewers* know that the characters' misapprehension is likely to be revealed at some later date.

A classic instance of this was the December, 1990, drowning death of Tad Martin on ABC's *All My Children*. The majority of characters believed he was dead, and those who didn't (such as his mother, Opal) had only a vague, quasi-mystical conviction that he had survived his fall into a river. Regardless of their hopes for his return, however, all the characters gradually picked up the threads of their lives on the assumption that he had died. Viewers, on the other hand, were certain that he was *not* dead, having seen an apparently amnesiac Tad getting into a truck after hitchhiking from New York to California. For several months, the show's producers actually hinted at his return by including his picture among the cast photographs shown during the opening credits and at commercial breaks. While there was no guarantee of exactly what would happen, viewers could reasonably expect that at some point Tad would return to Pine Valley—as indeed he did, in December, 1992.

Equivocation is a considerably more ambiguous gesture that also leaves open the possible future reemergence of a particular storyline, but it does so in a far less absolute way. For instance, if a character appears to have died but the body is not found, as happened (to take a random example) with Sharlene Hudson on NBC's *Another World* in 1993, it is possible that the character will reappear at some later date—as Sharlene in fact did in the spring of 1994. Such a return is not inevitable, however, and many conclusions that *seem* to be equivocal or ambiguous are actually only *potentially* so. (In other words, not all characters who die off-screen are resurrected later on.) Other conclusions may only be uncertain in retrospect, when a later storyline reveals that some apparently conclusive event did not fully resolve a problem. Indeed, soap opera writers often "retrofit" a lack of resolution and may even rewrite history, deciding sometimes years after the fact that a storyline was not definitively closed. (We may, for instance, have actually seen a dead body, only to discover somewhere down the road that it was misidentified. Think of all those previously unknown identical siblings and cousins.) In these cases, the viewer is, in a way, retrospectively "snared": Closure is in effect undone, reopened by being rewritten as false. (As Dorothy Hobson writes in her study of the British serial *Crossroads*, "the continuous narrative [of soap opera] means that although certain storylines may be resolved for the moment, there is always the possibility that mistakes can be rectified later and there is a potential for growth and change within the serial form.")[33]

I am talking here about something quite different from the familiar characterization of melodrama, which Jane Feuer has described as providing "an 'unsatisfying' or ambiguous sense of closure."[34] Feuer is drawing on an argument about the meanings of film melodrama that is often couched in terms of the genre's inability to close fully the ruptures it opens, particularly when it comes to ideological conceptions of women's sexuality, the family, romance, and so on. I will return later in this chapter to the particular ideological meanings that have been assigned to both closure and its lack, particularly in the case of soap opera, and to the ways in which various kinds of closure may be, in Feuer's terms, *ideologically* rather than simply narratively ambiguous. For the moment, at least, I want to separate a set of particular narrative strategies, procedures by which individual stories may be brought to a resolution, from the broader ideological implications of those procedures. I am interested here in a specific form of story resolution whose use is not necessarily tied to any particular story content or political position.

Although critics and theorists tend to see soap operas as generally characterized by *temporary* closure, this, too, should be seen as a very specific device. It occurs when a particular storyline's forward movement is briefly stopped without its essential components being fully resolved or its motivating question answered, as when a character suddenly goes out of town for no particular reason or when events that have been prominent are put aside and picked up again later on.[35] The most blatant example of this is the way in which individual episodes generally end,[36] but temporary closure has many other uses. Sometimes it is simply meant to permit characters to become quickly involved in new storylines that for some reason require immediate introduction, or to deal with events beyond the program (such as holiday celebrations or the need to recast a character when an actor suddenly leaves a show). At other times, a story may be put on hold to allow other figures to dominate the action, to make room for a spectacle like a wedding, or to accommodate the fact that another storyline is approaching resolution.[37]

This last role is especially important, for the suspension of one or more stories is commonly used as a device to highlight another storyline's movement toward or achievement of closure. Although soaps juggle multiple concurrent storylines, a single one often dominates as it nears a climax, while other, tangential stories—usually those involved in separate arcs—recede into the background or are put entirely on hold, with no narrative progression occurring for days or even weeks at a time. On rare occasions, developments related to a single storyline or, more commonly, a single arc will take up an entire episode. This was the case with the events immediately leading up to and resulting from Tad Martin's apparent death on *All My Children*, when for several episodes nothing occurred on-screen that was not directly related to his demise. On a smaller scale, *Another World* suspended its other storylines completely to devote a whole April 1991 episode to a confrontation between two characters, one of whom had shot the other.[38] And on *One Life to Live*, after months of almost daily development, Billy's coming-out story was put on the back burner shortly after the AIDS quilt visited Llanview.

What I call *series-style* closure may be easily mistaken for this sort of temporary suspension, and it contributes even more directly to the illusion that closure is never achieved. In this type, a storyline reaches a conventional resolution—a couple comes together or separates, a dispute is settled, a person reenters the family circle—but the continuing diegetic presence of the characters involved in the original problem leaves the way open for its future redevelopment. In terms of the forward movement of the soap opera narrative, the resolution is complete, for the question that initially propelled the storyline has been answered. Although the problem may reemerge, there is no specific reason to expect it to do so.

The most important aspect of this kind of closure, however, is the fact that, as long as the characters continue to exist, so too does the potential for further conflict between them. For instance, Adam Chandler and Brooke English of *All My Children* have "resolved" their relationship several times, but continue to reenact its basic problematic, which stems from the conflict between his need to control others and her stubborn independence. This is different, however, from the mere continued co-presence of characters who have little or no meaningful interaction (such as *All My Children*'s Erica Kane and her ex-husband Tom Cudahy), or whose ongoing relationship provides background for front-burner stories but is rarely featured in the narrative (such as *All My Children*'s Ruth and Joe Martin).

Series-style closure is distinct from both equivocation and temporary closure (where the resolutions themselves lack clarity), for its "temporariness" results directly from the continuing nature of the program, rather than from any uncertainty about the outcome of a particular storyline. As the name I have given it suggests, it closely resembles the kind of closure that occurs on conventional episodic television. The continuing situation and cast of characters on a prime-time sitcom, for example, leaves open the very real possibility that a problem that has been solved in one episode may recur in another. John Ellis contends that episodic TV never completely reaches resolution, offers indeed no real opportunity for the kind of full closure we know from novels. There is, he says, "no final closure to the series' own recurring problematic."[39] Although Ellis is talking about episodic television, he offers a description that is equally apt for soap operas: "Fundamentally, the series implies the form of the dilemma rather than that of resolution and closure. This perhaps is the central contribution that broadcast TV has made to the long history of narrative forms and narrativised perception of the world."[40] But to say that the television narrative is ultimately irresolvable is quite a different thing from insisting that there is no possibility for closure within a particular genre like the soap opera.

Soap operas' entangled storylines, plenitude of delaying strategies, and abundance of opportunities for closure challenge novice viewers' attempts to sort things out, yet the programs employ many standard conventions to signal the development of a particular story.[41] Among these are the increasing complications, tension, and momentum that experienced viewers easily recognize as marking a story's forward movement, as well as the device of suspending other storylines as a single one reaches its close, which I have already mentioned as an example of temporary closure. Such signs of imminent climax are by no means universal, but neither does their absence automatically indicate a lack of resolution. For that matter, storylines need not be concluded through direct, on-screen action. Some simply disappear (again, sometimes because of extratextual events, such as an actor's precipitous departure), their resolutions conducted off-screen and described or mentioned in passing by characters in ongoing stories. In other cases, the resolutions of minor stories, or of enigmas that never quite rise to the level of fully developed storylines, may be completely subsumed by the conclusions of the larger stories or even the arcs in which they are embedded. But regardless of how viewers learn of closure, both its anticipation and its eventual achievement play an important role in the way they watch the programs. This in turn has some crucial implications both for soap opera as a source of viewer pleasure and for the genre's role in ideology.

In *S/Z*, Roland Barthes argues that readers of narrative—and, by implication, consumers of visual narrative forms as well—are pulled along by a desire to reach the story's end, the point at which all of their questions will be answered, all the narrative enigmas disclosed.[42] Although they often depict this "desire" as a feature of the text itself, narrative theorists maintain that the anticipation of resolution exerts a magnetic attraction on those who consume a given narrative. Yet that desire also exists in constant tension with the pleasure of its deferral. According to Peter Brooks, "The desire of the text (the desire of reading) is hence desire for the end, but desire for the end reached only through the at least minimally complicated detour, the intentional deviance, in tension, which is the point of narrative."[43]

Film theorists like Stephen Neale have made similar arguments: "the wish for the narrative to continue is structured as directly in conflict with a wish for the representation of fulfilment of desire, while the wish for the narrative to end coherently is organised in conflict with a pleasure in the process of desire itself."[44] According to Neale, an individual genre "engages and structures differently the two basic subjective mechanisms . . .: the want for the pleasure of process and the want for the pleasure of its closure."[45] In other words, we long for closure, yet the progression toward it must be impeded and delayed in order to prolong the pleasure of viewing or reading. Without this postponement, after all, there would be no narrative, only synopsis.

The insistence on soaps' generic irresolution, however, has led critics to dismiss this aspect of narrative and look elsewhere for the sources of viewer pleasure. Since soaps are presumed not to achieve any meaningful sort of closure, perhaps it is the indefinite postponement, the waiting itself, that women enjoy.[46] But if postponement is in fact characteristic of all storytelling, we must either rethink the relationship between pleasure and the deferral of resolution or redefine soap operas' relation to narrative. One way out of this dilemma might be to conclude that soap operas are not narratives at all. Yet whether we choose the simplest definition of narrative—Cohan and Shires's "series of events in a temporal sequence"[47]—or a more complex one, such as Edward Branigan's "global interpretation of changing data measured through sets of relationships,"[48] soaps seem to fit the category.

There is more at stake here than questions about narrative pleasure. The traditional narrative drive toward closure has long been understood in ideological terms, and the argument over whether or not a particular form or genre achieves or even aspires to it thus carries some important freight. To begin with, film theorists have long linked narrative closure to a particular kind of ideological expression. Analyses of the realist tradition and of "classical" Hollywood cinema have often maintained that conventional closure works to reinforce dominant ideology at the levels of both content (by shutting off alternative futures that might disrupt the status quo) and structure (by insisting on a linear understanding of experience, promoting the notion of tidy solutions, and forcing viewers to accept a single interpretation of fictional events).[49]

Jane Feuer has summarized this view in her discussion of *Dallas* and *Dynasty*, contending that closure is "crucial to theories of textual deficiencies which run counter to the dominant ideology."[50] She is referring specifically to the familiar "argument that the 'happy endings' of Sirk's films fail to contain their narrative excess, allowing contradictions in the text to remain exposed" (p. 12). If we accept this claim about film, says Feuer, then we may conclude that, "[s]ince

[television] serials offer only temporary resolutions, . . . the teleo-
logical metaphysics of classical narrative structure have been subverted"
on programs like the prime-time serials she describes (p. 12).
As I indicated in chapter 2, I have profound doubts about the
degree to which the film category of melodrama can be applied to
television, but the idea that serial television's lack of closure can help
to undermine the ideological power of "classical narrative structure"
is a widely accepted one. In fact, many theorists have taken it a step
further, linking this potentially radical effect to the television apparatus itself, which Feuer herself describes as "work[ing] against logical
notions of causality and closure."[51] Caren Deming has in turn characterized television programs as "inherently incomplete,"[52] while John
Caughie theorizes that television narratives are structured around the
expectation of interruption rather than closure.[53]

Positions on the ideological function of closure in television have
been additionally complicated by recent ideas about the supposedly
oppositional nature of popular culture as form and practice.[54] So thoroughly have some television theorists absorbed not simply the association between closure and conservative ideology, but the idea that
the consumption of popular culture by nondominant groups is necessarily oppositional, that even writers who are attempting to define
the medium's uniqueness and forge a new, television-specific theory
seem unable to break the connection. Caren Deming, for instance,
argues precisely against applying film- and literature-based theoretical concepts to the study of television, but hints that even a critical
interest in closure is inherently conservative when she insists that traditional aesthetic standards "interpose themselves between television
critics and their subjects by valorising closure in the conceptualisation
of narrative."[55]

As Deming's essay demonstrates, the very question of closure's
existence has itself taken on a specific political cast. Some television
theorists concerned with gender have gone so far as to identify closure as a "masculine" narrative strategy and nonclosure—especially
as it occurs in soap opera—as a "feminine" one, and to categorize
programs and genres in those terms. (John Fiske, for instance, makes
this association throughout *Television Culture*, insisting that the
nonclosure of soap opera narratives is a major marker of "feminine"
programs.)[56] Because traditional resolution is theoretically tied to the

maintenance of the status quo, critics search for irresolution in the popular culture forms enjoyed by women and other nondominant groups. This partially explains, I think, the insistence that much of women's enjoyment of soap opera rests on the deferral of narrative resolution. If closure is "patriarchal," the implicit argument goes, then nonclosure must by definition be subversive; and because women are presumed to be oppositional viewers, those who enjoy a popular cultural form that appears to lack closure must enjoy it precisely because of that lack.

There are several serious flaws in this chain of thinking, particularly when it is applied to soap operas. First of all, it overlooks the fact that these programs are above everything else highly conventional products of commercial mass media designed specifically to capture an audience of potential consumers for the sponsors who support and, in some cases, actually produce the programs. Even if soap operas exhibit the features of, say, avant-garde feminist films that explicitly valorize nonlinearity, they do so within the context of commercial broadcast television—a context in which narrative strategies take on quite different roles from those they play within the avant-garde. To ignore this is to oversimplify the project of challenging dominant ideology. As Barbara Klinger has pointed out, "The designation of texts and genres as 'progressive' . . . . suggests that a disturbance in the system can be achieved sheerly through the intervention of invention."[57] But such a "disturbance" requires a far more complex "intervention" than that posed by the refusal of a specific narrative strategy like story resolution. At the very least, such an intervention would also have to occur at the level of content.[58] Yet, as most feminist analyses of soap opera have shown, these programs reinforce, not only male dominance in general, but the specific institutions that support and enable it. So prominent is this content, in fact, that it is difficult to understand exactly how patriarchal messages can be undermined by a simple lack of narrative closure.[59]

In addition, the assumption that when nonclosure is present it must be a—perhaps *the*—major source of pleasure, ignores the potentially pleasurable aspects of the rest of the soap opera apparatus, including the moments of resolution that interrupt what is at another level an interminable serial. Both Charlotte Brunsdon and Christine Geraghty have pointed out that viewers—including those of us who are critics and theorists—find real enjoyment in predicting future developments on their favorite soaps, regardless of the ideological content communicated by such developments. In Geraghty's words, "The pleasures of soaps are so much bound up with speculation and analysis that they demand that viewers share the experience."[60] And while Brunsdon distinguishes between the fun of generalized speculation and the enjoyment of watching a story being worked out in detail, she acknowledges that, as a viewer, "my pleasure . . . is in how my prediction comes true."[61] And such curiosity about outcome is not confined to theorists and critics; the proliferation of magazine and newspaper synopses of soap opera storylines testifies to an interest among nonprofessional viewers in the resolution of particular storylines.

Informed speculation about how narrative enigmas will be resolved probably accounts for a good deal of the enjoyment regular consumers derive from formula fiction of all sorts. Soap opera viewers are no doubt typical in negotiating between their curiosity about what will happen next and their understanding, gathered through experience of the form and the individual program, that certain outcomes are more likely than others. As they watch, viewers make educated guesses about how various mysteries and problems will be solved and how specific relationships will develop, while scriptwriters try to keep this anticipation from becoming straightforward prediction by surprising viewers with an unexpected revelation or even, on occasion, killing off a central character.[62]

An important lesson of feminist criticism and cultural studies is the recognition that viewers develop just such a dense and complex knowledge of both specific programs and the larger genre. But the knowledge they gain does not consist simply of memorized family trees, or even the recognition of formulaic conventions. They know, for example, that some shows take a stern view of all nonmarital sex, while others reserve direct punishment for adultery, and this knowledge encourages viewers to anticipate particular kinds of conclusions to particular storylines. They may not think of the stories in explicitly ideological terms, but fully competent viewers know that certain resolutions are more or less consistent with the "message" of the program(s) they watch.

In the realm of sexuality, for example, regular viewers of ABC's

All My Children and *General Hospital* know that both programs now permit unmarried couples to have sexual relationships without imposing crude forms of direct punishment, such as inevitable pregnancy or even scandal. *All My Children*, however, is far more "permissive" in this regard, often presenting unmarried adult couples who maintain lengthy sexual relationships, often without any clear commitment to marry (although adultery and affairs that violate particular age barriers are another question). *General Hospital*, on the other hand, tends to favor chastity for its characters, whether intentional (choosing to wait until marriage) or simply circumstantial (the couple never has an opportunity to be alone). *All My Children*'s gradual transformation of the sexually active Erica Kane into a relatively sympathetic character is almost unimaginable on *General Hospital*, where women like the sexually adventurous Bobbie Spencer must be rehabilitated into near-saints in order to become "good" characters. Thus, experienced viewers of *All My Children* may see nonmarital sexual activity as a morally neutral feature of a relationship between two characters, while *General Hospital* viewers can anticipate that some kind of trouble will result directly from it. (A similar dichotomy exists between, for instance, NBC's *Another World*, which permits "good" women characters to have ongoing sexual relationships outside of marriage, and CBS's *The Young and the Restless*, where chastity remains a mark of moral rectitude.) Such a difference in turn obviously influences the kinds of outcomes viewers predict for specific storylines.

The process by which viewers anticipate the resolutions of particular stories has implications that go far beyond our analysis of soap operas, for in addition to the ideological significance I have already discussed, closure has been understood as having a very specific function in the realm of discourse. Jerry Palmer summarizes a major school of thought when he describes closure as "the place where the meaning of events becomes fixed: no closure, no fixing of meaning."[63] And Fredric Jameson suggests how far that "fixing" may go when he writes: "not only does the *dénouement* . . . stand as the reified end in view of which the rest of the narrative is consumed—this reifying structure also reaches down in the very page-by-page detail of the book's consumption."[64] In other words, the moment of closure does not merely fix a text's meaning, it endows all that preceded it with a retrospective meaning, refiguring the entire text in terms of its ending, which now assumes a degree of inevitability it may or may not have possessed.

Yet the fact that viewers bring their experience of the genre as a whole and their knowledge of a specific program's history to bear on their consumption of an individual storyline necessarily enlarges our understanding of the role of the retrospective in narrative. Regular soap opera viewers necessarily understand every storyline in terms of the ones that preceded and overlap with it, and this includes their knowledge of how specific stories and general types of stories usually end. Even if we agree that "only the end can finally determine meaning,"[65] which end are we talking about when viewers use their experience of one story's conclusion to understand the meaning of the ones that follow?

If my earlier claim about the function of soap opera closure is correct—that its basic purpose is to free characters, and thus viewers, to become involved in new storylines—then the multiplying arcs of soap opera that create the serials' overall *irresolution* actually owe their existence, paradoxically, to the regular *resolution* of individual stories. Such resolutions serve to reconfigure a narrative that would otherwise be, not simply endless, but knee-deep in impossibly complicated storylines.

As crucial as this structural purpose is, however, closure has another major function for soap opera narrative. As we will see in the next chapter, the stories themselves may disrupt or threaten male dominance, but their resolutions are almost always in line with the ideology of capitalist patriarchy—reasserting the value of traditional marriage, for instance, or establishing patrilineage as a necessary component of identity—and this is where I want to locate soap opera closure's most important *ideological* work.

I want to stress once again that it is the specific *content* of the moments of closure, the way that individual story resolutions insist on the correctness of the patriarchal status quo and women's position within it, that accomplish this work, rather than the mere fact of resolution. Yet I do not mean to suggest that closure is merely a "hollow form" and that meaning resides entirely outside of such textual gestures.[66] Meaning is shaped at least in part by the use of specific narrative strategies, with closure an especially powerful way by which meaning can be fixed because it restricts possible fictional futures. In principle, closure could be easily turned to oppositional ends and stories could be resolved in ways that demonstrate, say, a wide range of romantic and sexual alternatives to heterosexual monogamy, or a variety of familial structures. Yet this does not happen in soap operas, where the form is made to serve existing power relations by expressing particular, highly formalized, constantly repeated fictional outcomes.

Specifically, these outcomes state and restate the moral imperatives of the genre as it is currently constituted on and by commercial U.S. television: Heterosexual love within a committed monogamous relationship (ideally marriage) is preferable to all other possible romantic relationships, with nonmonogamy always configured as betrayal. The traditional patrilineal family represents the only bulwark against loneliness and chaos, work serves mainly as a distraction from the far more important personal sphere of life, and no amount of money, success, glamour, fame, or sexual satisfaction can compensate characters who do not find romantic love and a secure place in a family. Secrets and unexpressed emotions necessarily lead to disaster in a community intimately implicated in every aspect of its members' lives, yet friendship is always secondary to familial and romantic ties.

Closure is by no means the only strategy used to express these messages. Characterization and performance styles, for instance, help to identify individuals who resist or exist outside of traditional social structures as inadequate, emotionally unbalanced, evil, and in other ways "deviant," particularly in the figures of sexually autonomous villainesses. In fact, the very choice of story subjects—heterosexuality but almost never homosexuality, family conflicts but rarely the political process—expresses an ideological agenda. Yet closure exerts an especially powerful force by drawing stories to a conclusion with events that reinforce the essential rightness of the programs' moral and ideological rules, that lend a sense of inevitability to the status quo and suggest that certain outcomes necessarily follow from certain behavior.[67] Women who put work before love will never find marital happiness; people who lie will always be found out.

As I will demonstrate in chapter 5, soap opera stories may allow women to fantasize about a world in which they have, for instance, the power to define the family, but these essentially utopian fantasies are regularly undermined by resolutions that restate the prevailing ideology.[68] Closure thus helps to manage women's discontent—and so their potential rebellion—and to reinforce patriarchy and the related oppressions of racism, classism, and heterosexism. While Brunsdon and Geraghty are probably correct in suggesting that viewing pleasure arises from confirming the accuracy of one's guesses about the future, the fact that the stories themselves work to express a conservative ideology means that, ironically, a major component of viewer pleasure involves seeing that ideology confirmed over and over again.

5

Plotting Paternity: Looking for Dad on the Daytime Soaps

> Entertainment is not primarily a vehicle for the transmission of ideas. But even the most emotionally saturated entertainment will also produce ideas, and these will certainly be locatable in terms of ideology.
>
> —Terry Lovell, "Ideology and *Coronation Street*"

■ As anyone familiar with the genre knows, the attribution of paternity is something of an obsession on daytime soap operas. In fact, if the frequency of unplanned pregnancies (often from a single sexual encounter), the prominence of storylines involving secrets or mistakes over paternity, and the importance characters attach to discovering who has fathered a particular child are any evidence, the preoccupation with questions and mysteries about paternity is almost a defining characteristic of the genre. Every single daytime soap opera, as well as each prime-time serial, deals with the issue of paternity on a regular basis, and the most heavily freighted single piece of information on any given show is commonly the knowledge of paternity. From a feminist perspective, the issue seems almost overdetermined—so much so that, if it is possible to describe soap operas as being "about" any one thing, they are about paternity.

The predominance of this subject, which is presented through what I call the *paternity plot*, raises a number of questions about how and why women viewers enjoy soap operas, and about the genre's political and ideological role. In particular, it is a paradigmatic example of the methods by which soap operas provide competent viewers with an opportunity for pleasurable anticipation and utopian, woman-centered fantasy, while ultimately containing and managing the disruptive aspects of that fantasy through the inevitable reestablishment of patriarchal order.

Before considering how this happens, let me briefly sketch the way paternal identity itself functions in feminist theory. This is in no way a thorough examination of feminist interpretations of paternity, but rather, an outline of the ideas that some feminist theorists have expressed about the meanings of fatherhood. Such analyses of the historical, social, and psychological significance of paternity can provide a useful ground against which to read the soap opera paternity plot. In addition, although I would not want to argue that all soap opera viewers are always thinking consciously about the cultural meanings of paternity while they watch the programs, those meanings do circulate through both discourse and social practice. Whether or not they bring them directly to bear on the shows they consume, culturally competent viewers understand paternity's social significance, and that understanding provides one of the lenses through which they interpret soap opera narratives.

For many feminist theorists concerned with the origins of women's oppression, the prehistoric discovery by men of their role in reproduction is a key moment.[1] Before the recognition of paternity, by some accounts, women were assumed to reproduce on their own or in concert with deities or nature, and were consequently viewed with awe. The power to create life seemed to put women on a par with other aspects of the natural world, and to position them above men, who appeared to be the only ones unable to exercise this creativity. Once men's role was discovered, however, this interpretation of women's reproductive capacity dissolved, and new rituals evolved that emphasized men's importance, including the development of elaborate kinship networks that depended on exogamy.[2] Efforts to prove that men were the "true"—that is, the culturally significant—parents extended to biological explanations of reproduction, and attempts persisted well into the scientific age to demonstrate that women were merely vessels for *men's* magical ability to create life.[3]

This view of women's symbolic fall from reproductive power does not fully explain the oppression of women, but there is no doubt about men's anxiety over the question of paternity. As many feminist theorists have pointed out, this anxiety springs from the fact that no man can ever be as certain of his children's identity as is the woman who bears them: only mothers know beyond any doubt that their children are their own. (It is important to note that changes in reproductive technology could ultimately place women in the same position as men in this regard. Even as social relationships like surrogacy increasingly complicate the legal definition of motherhood, embryo transplants and other techniques are likely to complicate the biological meanings of parenthood for both sexes.) Fatherhood is, in this sense, a myth, an ultimately unprovable claim that we agree to accept as fact.[4] Elaborate legal, social, and religious barriers have been raised in an attempt to ensure the "fact" of paternity, but the very existence of these regulations only serves to underline the profound anxiety that surrounds the issue. In the words of Mary Ann Doane,

> Paternity and its interrogation . . . are articulated within the context of . . . *social* legitimacy. To generate questions about the existence of one's father is, therefore, to produce an insult of the highest order. . . . Knowledge of maternity is constituted in terms of immediacy. . . . Knowledge of paternity, on the other hand, is mediated—it allows of gaps and invisibilities, of doubts in short. It therefore demands external regulation in the form of laws governing social relations. . . .[5]

Soap operas speak directly to the anxiety that demands such regulation, demonstrating the uncertainty of paternity in endlessly repeated storylines. But these stories do not just stir up anxiety. They inevitably resolve it by reenacting the discovery that men—specific men— are fathers. Soaps thus perform what Thomas Elsaesser and others have called a "myth-making" function,[6] and although there is rarely any such guarantee in real life, the question of soap opera fatherhood is always given a definite answer.

In the preceding chapter, I argued that a wide range of resolving gestures and strategies for closure occur within soap opera, but only one—traditional full closure—need concern us here. That is because definitive resolution is one of the paradigmatic characteristics of what I have defined as the paternity plot. The plot itself rests on a simple premise: a woman character becomes pregnant but does not know or will not reveal the father's identity. The storyline generally begins at or just before conception, but such a beginning may only be implicit, since some paternity plots, particularly the ones involving the sudden appearance of previously unknown adult children, only erupt many years after the fact. Other characters—usually including but never limited to the men who might have fathered her child—become involved in the pregnancy or with the child, depending on the stage at which the mystery becomes known. According to their relationships to the woman and in keeping with their functions as "good" or "evil" figures, these characters attempt to discover, repress, or reveal the pregnancy's origin. Predictable soap opera complications ensue and varying lengths of time may pass between conception and revelation, but the identity of the true father eventually becomes public knowledge. There are numerous variations on this basic plot, the most common of which revolve around the woman's engagement or marriage to a man other than the lover responsible for her pregnancy, that lover's marriage or engagement to another woman, or—in the case of adult children—rivalry between legitimate or acknowledged offspring and their newly discovered (putative) sibling.[7]

The paternity plot is so pervasive that examples can be chosen almost at random, but one should be enough to suggest the mechanisms by which it is typically worked out. In the spring of 1994, *All My Children* revealed that Dimitri Marrick had unknowingly fathered a son in Hungary by one of his family's servants, Corvina Lane, over 20 years earlier. Corvina had raised the child, Anton, as her brother, and while Anton had been living in Pine Valley for some months, his true identity was only discovered when Dimitri's brother and sister-in-law Edmund and Maria, honeymooning at the Marricks' Hungarian estate, found a cryptic old unsent letter from Corvina to Dimitri and confronted Corvina about her secret. Although they soon informed Dimitri of his real relationship with Anton, for whom he had always felt a special but heretofore unexplained fondness, Corvina strenuously objected to telling Anton that she and Dimitri were his parents, leaving the four characters who were in the know struggling to keep the information away, not only from Anton, but from his conniving fiancee, Kendall.

Typically, the Marrick family history is a tangle of stories about mysterious paternity and maternity: Kendall is the previously unknown daughter of Dimitri's estranged wife, Erica Kane, and the discovery that Edmund is Dimitri's brother was itself the center of an elaborate, Gothic-style paternity plot. Such complex family trees and the tension and suspense that surround them may be relatively rare in real life, but the ubiquitousness of the paternity plot makes them typical of kinship relations on soap operas, where most members of a family like the Marricks have been involved in some kind of paternity mystery.

Significantly, however, while the immediate effects of such mysteries are profound, it is also rare for such a dispute to resonate very far beyond the revelation of the true father. Although post-revelation resentment occasionally lasts a few weeks (or a few months on prime-time shows), the tension is focused on the actual news about paternity, and it is a rare soap opera character who continues to harbor negative feelings beyond the moment of confrontation and acknowledgment. (For example, although much drama surrounded the revelation itself, once *All My Children*'s Adam Chandler acknowledged Hayley Vaughan as his daughter, Hayley adjusted quickly to the new relationship, and soon began characterizing the manipulative Adam as a good father.) When such resentment does last longer, it tends to be a function of the resentful character's already well-established "evil," selfish, or spiteful nature. (On *One Life to Live*, Tina Lord's transformation from an evil and conniving character to a more sympathetic one was marked in part by her shift from resentment to acceptance of the identity of her father, the late Victor Lord.) Despite the fact that it initially threatens to destroy the family structure, then, the paternity mystery is in practice only a temporary disruption of family life, one whose long-term effects consist almost entirely of the realignment of specific family ties, rather than the undermining of essential family or community frameworks.

Although it is easiest to focus on fairly recent examples, I want to note at the outset that the paternity plot has been a fixture in soap operas at least since their earliest days on television. Less than six months after *The Guiding Light* became the first radio soap to move to television, writer Irna Phillips was planning a storyline in which Kathy Lang Grant, pregnant by her dead first husband, tried to attribute the baby to her second husband.[8] Regular soap opera viewers will be able to come up with many other examples of paternity mysteries on long-running serials like *General Hospital* and NBC's *Another World*. Programs that have been on the air long enough to allow multiple generations to be born and grow up inevitably contain adult characters whose mysterious paternity provided plot interest in the 1950s, 1960s, and 1970s. (For instance, the Tara-Chuck-Phil love triangle which reigned when ABC's *All My Children* began in 1970 as a soap featuring adolescents led eventually to an elaborate paternity plot, and although the mystery was settled years ago, the child in question, Charlie Brent, is now a recurring adult character.)

The repeated eruption of storylines that center on questionable paternity is striking on statistical grounds alone, but an even more telling aspect of this chain of secrecy and revelation is the fact that paternity can always be proven absolutely. Although it may seem to the casual viewer that the women characters are so promiscuous that they cannot be sure who has fathered their children, it almost always turns out that any given woman knows the truth. She has lied about having an affair, was actually pregnant earlier or later than other characters realized, or for some other reason can demonstrate that there is no real question. If all else fails, blood tests are infallible—assuming that no one bribes the lab technicians or tampers with the computer records. Although in real life such tests have until recently only been able to prove who is *not* the father, on soap operas they have long proven paternity beyond dispute, even when the choice has been between close relatives. The recent incorporation of new technologies like DNA testing (used in February, 1992, for instance, to prove Sean Donely's relationship to his son Conner on *General Hospital*) thus merely provides up-to-date scientific support for well-established soap opera fact.

On the surface, such storylines seem to fit easily into the daytime soaps' fixation on their characters' private lives. As Tania Modleski has pointed out, soap operas' preoccupation with private questions— family, love, sex, loyalty, jealousy—reassures the traditional daytime audience of home-centered women that their focus on the private world is not merely legitimate, but fascinating.[9] By presenting not only women, but men who are as bound up with private concerns as the most stereotypical housewife, these programs glamorize those interests and reassure viewers that such men do—or could—exist. (Janice Radway makes an analogous point about the male heroes of romance novels, who can be seen at their first appearance to express a "feminine" sensitivity that she suggests contrasts with the men in romance readers' daily lives.)[10] This characterization of the shows' bias toward the private explains their almost exclusive focus on the family, and the elision of public and private I outlined in chapter 3 explains the fact that every member of the soap opera community eventually discovers the secrets of paternal identity.

Still, we might expect that, for home-centered women viewers, issues of *maternity* would be far more compelling than issues of paternity. And indeed, there are cases in which maternity is in question—often involving babies switched at birth—although it is not a common plot device. For example, many years ago on *One Life to Live*, well-meaning friends told a former prostitute that her baby had died and gave the child to a former nun, who did not know that her baby *had* died. (Although paternity plots figure prominently on this show, the writers of *One Life to Live* also seem to be unusually interested in cases of mistaken or unknown maternity. Two separate maternity mysteries were featured during 1989 alone, one a particularly complicated storyline involving the recovery by Viki Lord Buchanan of a daughter born to her 25 years earlier, the other a version of the standard baby-switching plot. Viki's story was especially complex because her multiple personality disorder and resultant partial amnesia meant that she was unaware of the existence of her daughter Megan.) Like paternity mysteries, maternity mysteries are always resolved through the absolute identification of the mother and/or child, yet the very rarity of this plot twist highlights the extent to which uncertainties and anxieties about *men's* position within the family are manipulated and reversed in soap operas.

Why, however, does paternity figure so prominently in a genre directed primarily at women? A simple but inadequate explanation, of course, is that mainstream, mass-media-generated popular culture reflects the prevailing political and social ethos of the culture in which it is produced, in this case patriarchal interests that privilege the father's role and identity over the mother's. But a consideration of the differences between soap opera presentations of uncertain maternity and paternity may help to illuminate the choice to emphasize the latter.

First of all, the paternity plot is narratively both far simpler and far richer in potential complications than one centered on mistaken or unknown maternity. For a child's father to be unknown, no intentional act of deception is needed. It is only necessary for a woman character to have had or appear to have had sex with more than one man around the time of conception. Although the woman herself may be actively plotting to conceal the information, or to pin the pregnancy on an "innocent" man, there are many other possible explanations, including an unreported rape, a secret love affair, or that time-honored soap staple, the sudden return of a long-lost husband or lover. This is largely a narrative consideration, but it helps to explain why such a theme would prove popular among soap opera writers. While simplicity of premise is not necessarily the overriding concern, extremely complicated plots do not often become staples. Since a daily serial quickly exhausts new story ideas, this wide range of possible explanations and the suspense inherent in them makes paternity an excellent subject for a continuing serial in which additional storylines must constantly be introduced. Questions about a character's paternity can be introduced at any time, even "retrofitted" years later.[11]

In contrast, the physical facts of reproduction make maternity a relatively less abundant source of either suspense or mystery. For a child's *mother* to be unknown, someone must act—and act after the child's birth—to confuse or obscure things. Although it is possible for the error to be innocent, and thus not part of an explicit plot to confound identity or custody, it cannot be truly inadvertent. And because maternal identity itself cannot usually be as mysterious as paternity, it is far more difficult to introduce the idea of questionable maternity after the fact and there are probably fewer potential permutations to a maternity-centered plot. While such secrets are not unheard of, it is far more difficult for a woman to hide a pregnancy than for a man to conceal a sexual liaison, and it is far easier to prove, whether through eyewitness testimony or medical examination, that a woman has given birth than that a man has fathered a child.

The easiest way to understand the differences between maternity and paternity plots is to contrast two storylines that centered on suspicions or discoveries of parental identity. On CBS's *The Young and the Restless*, a previously existing paternity plot about Victor Newman's putative son by his former secretary, Eve Howard, reerupted in early 1993. While acknowledging the brief sexual relationship that might have led to Eve's pregnancy, Victor had refused for years to take her attribution of paternity seriously, but his recent estrangement from his legitimate children and their mother, his ex-wife Nikki, aroused Victor's curiosity about Eve's son Cole, an aspiring writer. Without telling anyone in the family about Cole's possible identity, Victor installed him at the Newman ranch, home not only to Nikki, but to Victoria and Nicholas, her children by Victor. Although Victor's original plan was to use this proximity to get to know Cole and decide for himself whether to claim him as a son—and the potential heir to his vast fortune—other events soon intervened to remove Victor from the scene. In his absence, Victoria's secret but growing sexual attraction to Cole threatened to develop into an incestuous relationship, while Nikki's similar attraction to him set up a sexual rivalry that ultimately shattered the bonds between mother and daughter. The story of Cole's uncertain paternity thus focused, typically, on the complications that ensue when a member of the soap opera community is not clearly positioned within the traditional patrilineal family. In this case, Victoria and Cole fell in love, married, and, unlike some other characters in similar situations, actually consummated their marriage, only to discover soon afterwards that they were apparently sister and brother. A pregnancy scare and an annulment followed, but DNA testing eventually proved that Victor was not in fact Cole's father, and the couple remarried.

Compare an *All My Children* storyline about Erica's discovery of her daughter Kendall, which developed at about the same time as this *Young and the Restless* story. Kendall's birth was the result of rape, an event Erica and her mother Mona had for more than 20 years kept secret from everyone, including their various husbands and lovers and Erica's other daughter, Bianca. Kendall, however—put up for adoption at birth and embittered by her biological mother's apparent rejection—eventually tracked Erica down and demanded recognition of their relationship. Although she acknowledged Kendall soon after realizing who she was, the sudden appearance of the daughter conceived through rape forced Erica to relive the trauma, in nightmares and in repeated descriptions of the experience, and the subsequent storyline followed two paths: Erica's efforts to explain the circumstances of her pregnancy and her reasons for keeping Kendall's existence a secret, and Kendall's attempts to ingratiate herself with Erica and intimidate Bianca, whom she saw as usurping her own rightful place as Erica's first child.

One obvious difference between the Erica/Kendall maternity story and the Victor/Cole paternity story has to do with their narrative focuses. The former is a story necessarily based on intentional concealment—of the rape, of Kendall's existence—while the latter is a story about uncertain identity: Is Cole really Victor's son and if so, what is Cole's relationship to everyone else in the community? Yet the differences between the *meanings* of maternity and paternity are emphasized by the quite different degrees of catastrophe that threaten to erupt within those stories. Kendall's existence endangers many characters' happiness—especially Erica's and Bianca's—and Erica's revisitation of her rape is quite traumatic, but because of the potentially incestuous relationship between Cole and Victoria, Cole's presence carries with it the potential to destroy Victor's entire family.

Once again, of course, the basis of these distinctions between maternity and paternity plots is likely to change as reproductive technologies such as embryo transplants and in vitro fertilization find a permanent place in soap opera plots. Although adoption and adultery have been the soaps' traditional solutions to characters' fertility problems, changes in the social and technological relations of reproduction will no doubt mean changes in fictional "solutions" as well. (Both *All My Children* and *General Hospital* have already made use of surrogacy plots, and *One Life to Live* has already employed an embryo transplant.) It is easy to imagine a future maternity plot whose central mystery is whether a pregnancy was the result of an embryo transplant or "normal" conception.

As the example of the Newman family suggests, the difference between unknown mothers and fathers goes far beyond the writers' need to come up with potentially intriguing storylines. After all, this particular plot formula takes place in a fictional context which consistently presents pregnancy and maternity as passive conditions, and one of the most obvious tactics for establishing this passivity is rhetorical. Women characters almost always describe themselves (and are described by others) as "carrying" their lovers' children. This description seems most prominent when a woman is pregnant by a man who is for some reason unavailable to her (usually because he is married to someone else), so that it may express the woman's willingness to settle for the small part of him she possesses through his child. But even more important, it implies that the woman sees herself as a passive receptacle for the more active male progenitor.

The rhetoric of soap operas also has women "giving" children to men, a dramatic verbal admission of who controls the family. Although this may suggest a certain degree of activity (versus merely "carrying" a child), it is activity in the service of passivity, so to speak, rather than real active agency. By positioning a woman in the role of recipient, an August, 1989, episode of *General Hospital* incidentally highlighted the rhetoric by which a woman "carries" a child for another parent. When Bobbie Spencer Meyer accidentally discovered the identity of the woman whose baby she was waiting to adopt, her conversation with the adoption agency representative included a question about when she had discovered that this woman was carrying "her" (i.e., Bobbie's) child.

Added to this rhetorical characterization of pregnancy as a passive activity is the remarkable fact that few soap opera women seem able to recognize the symptoms of pregnancy on their own, but must be diagnosed by a (usually male) doctor. They frequently go to the doctor because of vague or mysterious symptoms—faintness, nausea, fatigue—but almost never does a woman note a missed period and deduce her own condition. (This is, of course, perfectly in keeping with soap opera women's striking ignorance of their own reproductive systems, including their apparent lack of information about or access to contraception and their constant surprise at unplanned pregnancies.) Thus, despite other instances of active agency, the presentation of pregnancy on the soaps highlights women's passivity. In fact, activity and awareness of pregnancy are often associated with villainy; "evil" women characters frequently plot to become pregnant in order to exert control over a man, and often claim to know they are pregnant immediately.

The soaps' treatment of abortion and miscarriage is also relevant here. Miscarriage is unrealistically frequent on soap operas, and often occurs under truly ridiculous circumstances (as on *General Hospital* many years ago, when a character was pregnant for 14 months and finally miscarried in a fall down the stairs). Abortion is virtually always wrong, even in cases of rape, and this judgment frequently turns openly on the inappropriateness of a woman's autonomous decision to abort. Other characters—including men not directly involved in the pregnancy—may interfere by telling the would-be father, who attempts to prevent the abortion; or the woman may be struck with sudden feelings of guilt as she is about to undergo the procedure. It is worth noting the rare exceptions to soaps' stern no-abortion code—from Brooke English's post-rape abortion in the 1970s on *All My Children*, to Ashley Abbott's late-1980s termination of her pregnancy by Victor Newman on *The Young and the Restless*, to Ellie Anderson's 1992 abortion on CBS's *As the World Turns*—since they actually serve to reinforce the very prohibition they seem to undermine. If the abortion takes place, the woman is almost always assailed by regret afterward, often accompanied by the imagined crying of babies (Ashley), and inevitably, the would-be father sees the abortion as a betrayal of his rights to the child (as happened both with Victor and with Ellie's husband Kirk). On the extremely rare occasion when a man actually wants a woman to have an abortion, this too is couched in a way that identifies the procedure as anything but her autonomous choice. (A 1993 storyline on *The Young and the Restless*, for instance, temporarily reversed the conventional terms when John Abbott demanded that his wife Jill abort a pregnancy she had planned against his express wishes, but both the intentional pregnancy and Jill's faked abortion followed the standard path of female manipulation and deceit in the face of male attempts to control women's reproductive experiences.)

The "immorality" of abortion provides a logical counterpoint to the prominence of plots about women unable to become pregnant or carry a child to term. But beyond this, both the highly charged negative portrayal of abortion and the alarming frequency of miscarriages support the soaps' insistence on pregnancy as something that *happens to* women, and whose end is beyond their control. This aspect of women's passivity is emphasized by the fact that the decision over abortion is frequently rendered moot when a woman considering the procedure conveniently experiences a miscarriage. It is also likely, however, that extratextual considerations are at work here, namely writers' and producers' unwillingness to present abortion as a positive choice in the context of an intense social debate over women's reproductive rights. Convenient miscarriage permits them to entertain the possibility of abortion without actually having to approve or reject it.

It is easy to see why voluntary abortion should be so threatening in a fictional world in which men have invested great significance in family life, for a woman who willingly terminates a pregnancy also terminates a tie with the would-be father and cuts off his power to control the situation, the woman, and the child to come. The fact that, through abortion, a woman can intervene to forestall permanently a man's ability to exert control makes abortion an exercise of real power (as it may sometimes be in real life), and thereby gives significance to the nearly uniform soap opera rejection of this choice as a moral one. Thus it is consistent that there are only two "appropriate" conclusions to a soap opera pregnancy: carrying a baby to term or inadvertently miscarrying. The other obvious choice, a voluntary abortion, represents an active exertion of control by the pregnant woman that violates her identification as passive.

This connection is underlined by the way that "evil" women characters who want to trap a man into marriage, or at least the acknowledgment of paternity, often play on the issue of control by threatening abortion. This is just one instance in which villainesses demonstrate their understanding of the soap opera "rules." Women viewers may, of course, read quite different lessons in the continuing struggle between good and evil, and may identify in some way with the manipulative villainesses.[12] I would argue, however, that the very fact that such women are identified as villainesses within the programs' narratives highlights the soaps' equation of "proper" femininity and passivity, at least within the framework set up by the narratives themselves.

The question then becomes why control in this particular area is so important. We might begin to answer this question by recognizing that on the soaps, as in real life, paternity is more than a biological fact. It means inheritance of name and property, defines kinship patterns, and seems to carry the weight of loyalty, family traits, and even day-to-day behavior. On soap operas, the assimilation of all family members into the family of the father is so complete that, for example, a woman who marries into a family often takes on whatever traits are typical of the new family. (On countless occasions on *Gen-*

eral Hospital, for instance, Monica Quartermaine has been referred to as a "real" Quartermaine, although she carries that name and identity only through her marriage to Alan.)

The fact that inheritance of wealth and property is so frequently the key to attributions and misattributions of paternity suggests that for many soap opera women, the power to name the father represents a concrete form of economic power. Although the attribution of paternity is often presented in terms of love, it is also often a question of money: If he thinks (or knows) this child is his, he'll have to marry me and give my child his name, money, and position. Or, from the child's point of view, the concealment of my father's identity has denied me access to money and power that are mine by right.

But the correct assignment of name and kinship position appears to be even more important, for questionable or misattributed paternity occurs even among soap opera characters of relatively modest means. When we remember soap operas' focus on private life and their construction of a closely knit community, the reason for this becomes clear: If the family is the most important structure in the world of the soaps, a character's relationship to a particular family is a central pole of his or her identity. Despite the use of workplace settings and the relatively recent introduction of exotic mystery and suspense plots, romantic and family relationships and conflicts remain the storyline staples, and such conflicts make the exact definition of a character's position in the family crucial. Just how important it is for soap opera characters to know their precise kinship positions is underlined by the occasional threat of brother-sister incest posed by unknown or misattributed paternity—as occurred, for instance, not only in the *Young and the Restless* Cole-Victor storyline, but when, in 1989, Cricket Blair and her half-brother Scott Grainger fell in love on the same show, and several years earlier, on *All My Children,* between Erica Kane and her half-brother Mark Dalton.[13]

In the soap opera world, the power to define another person's family position is often the only power women are permitted to exercise with impunity, and the only exertion of power that generates even short-term satisfaction. Although women characters wield other forms of power—through money, ownership of property or businesses, political influence, and so on—these women are usually villainesses, and they have often acquired financial or political power through marriage, divorce, or, more commonly, widowhood. "Good" women—even those who are wealthy and/or fully employed outside the home—exert power indirectly, primarily through family ties and most often by their private influence on other family members. This makes the ability to name and thereby control the father and define the family a crucial route to autonomy, however limited and temporary it may be.

The same larger context that identifies women's reproductive role as passive also defines soap opera women as dependent creatures. Women characters almost never achieve money, success, or political power through their own exertions, and if they do, it becomes insignificant in contrast to their unhappy personal lives. (Erica Kane is an archetypal example of this.) With few exceptions, women who would in the real world be seen as highly successful (such as prominent doctors and lawyers) expend all of their emotional energy sorting out their marriages, and seem to get little satisfaction and almost no public acclaim for their hard-won careers. In contrast, the men who seem so caught up in personal concerns continue at the same time to advance in their careers and to receive recognition and rewards for their performance in the public sphere.

The equation of paternity with inheritance and name is particularly noticeable on prime-time serials, largely because programs like *Dallas* tend to emphasize money and power over the daytime soaps' focus on love and family. While Elsaesser's suggestion, that melodrama is particularly adept at reproducing "the patterns of domination and exploitation existing in a given society, especially the relation between psychology, morality and class-consciousness," is an apt description of the power differentials implicit in daytime soap operas' gender relations, that characterization is almost transparently appropriate to the prime-time serials' obsession with financial power.[14] On *Dallas*, for example, family feelings—loyalty, say, as exemplified in the Barnes-Ewing feud—are couched almost entirely in terms of money and power, although lip service is paid to the importance of romantic love, respect for ties of blood, and so on. Because the show actually revolves around the central "character" of Ewing Oil, other bonds tend to be subordinated to the maintenance of the oil company. The families—both the Barneses and the Ewings—*are* their financial interests, and in this context, naming the father (as in the questionable paternity of John Ross Ewing and Pamela Barnes, among others) resonates with particular strength.

But as I've already suggested, the attribution of paternity is not only a function of power and money, for fatherhood is more than a social or economic role. Daytime soaps also posit an almost mystical bond between biological parents, and most notably, between father and child. (In the words of *The Young and the Restless*'s Nikki Reed Newman Abbott, "Once you've had children with someone, you're just naturally interested in what happens to them. . . . It's human nature.")[15] Western culture tends to promote the idea that *mothers* and children experience such a bond, and recent feminist theory has paid particular attention to the mother-child relationship.[16] But the focus of the soap opera paternity plot is, fittingly for a mainstream product of patriarchal culture, the profound feelings that *fathers* experience. A man's discovery that he has fathered a child arouses a powerful sense of love and attachment, frequently drawing him to the child's mother—often regardless of his previous feelings for her or his ties to any other woman—and almost always drawing him to the newly recognized child. (In contrast, for example, to Dimitri Marrick's affection for Anton, which preexisted his discovery of their biological relationship, Erica expressed great concern over the fact that her realization that Kendall was her daughter did *not* prompt an upsurge of maternal emotion.) The soap opera assertion of the power exerted by all family ties is evident here, but such a plot invests paternal feelings with a special kind of significance and weight. For instance, the child may be presented as forcing a couple to admit their love for one another, but such "love" is frequently indistinguishable from lack of interest or even dislike before the pregnancy. Shared parenthood is sometimes even capable of overcoming all other considerations, including infidelity or other betrayals, and couples not only get married and stay together because of a child, they often stay *happily* married—or as happily married as the exigencies of the soaps permit.

The positing of this special bond between fathers and their children may be an important source of pleasurable fantasy for women viewers all too aware that, if the statistics on child-support payments are any indication, men in the "real" world do not universally feel (much less express) such attachment. Thus, it is possible to see the soap opera version of fatherhood as a particularly "feminized" one. Needless to say, however, the depth of fathers' feelings toward their children is never the route to a feminist transformation of the soap opera family into one characterized by equal parenting or a sharing of domestic responsibilities. Although soap opera men are obsessed with private concerns, this obsession never extends to an interest in the maintenance work that family life requires. (Of course, few soap opera women not clearly marked as working class actually perform this work either, and such domestic labor as is performed on-screen is usually done by housekeepers or other domestic helpers. Nevertheless, soap opera women are presented as bearing primary responsibility for the domestic routine through their planning of parties, dinners, and holiday gatherings, and their direct supervision of household staff.)

As I argued in chapter 3, soap operas posit a community in which every event has the potential for endless repercussions. The programs always feature elaborate family crises that threaten to embroil all members, but the supposed bond between father and child makes the revelation of paternity perhaps the most extreme case. The impact of paternity extends beyond the lives of the would-be parents and their relatives. Weddings are canceled and relationships ended because of it. "How can I marry you when another woman is carrying your child!" exclaims the soap opera bride-to-be (usually on her wedding day, since suspense demands that this information be revealed at the last possible moment). Regardless of the circumstances surrounding conception, the discovery of a pregnancy almost always interrupts ongoing relationships because the creation of a child equals the creation of a bond between parents. Significantly, even when the father or father-to-be claims to feel nothing for the woman he has impregnated, his would-be wife often *insists* on the primacy of the biological father-mother-child triad. This is especially true if the wife or fiancee is herself unable to bear children, and indicates the success with which "good" soap opera women have absorbed the soap community's prevailing wisdom.

The mystique of the father-child bond is also demonstrated when a woman lies about a pregnancy or about her child's paternity in an attempt to force a man to marry her. Such situations usually rest on the woman's desire to make a man fall in love with her (although sometimes marriage alone is the goal), and her conviction that this will happen is one of the most stubborn feelings on the soaps. On *All My Children*, for instance, Natalie Hunter, pregnant by her recently deceased husband, claimed that her stepson and former lover Jeremy was actually the father, and insisted beyond all reason that his feelings for the child would lead inevitably to love for her. As always, a blood test resolved everything, but until that moment, no other arguments could persuade her that her belief was groundless—including Jeremy's obvious hatred of her, his commitment to another woman, and his suspicion (correct, as the audience knew) that he and Natalie had not actually had sex. Such insistence clearly draws on the folk convention that intense hatred is actually a cover for love. The fact that this sometimes turns out to be true for soap opera characters makes it even more significant that "true love" never follows from a woman's lies about pregnancy or paternity.

These twists will all be familiar to any regular soap opera viewer. But the fact that, year after year, soap opera women intentionally misattribute paternity brings us back to the question of why a television genre directed primarily at women should emphasize fatherhood rather than motherhood. One plausible explanation is simply that these plots offer viewers an opportunity for the vicarious experience of power, permitting women simultaneously to acknowledge and to manage feelings of powerlessness and emotional deprivation, a function Janice Radway suggests is also performed by romance novels.[17] In contrast to the traditional male-dominated family of real life, where power resides in the husband/father, the soap opera family confers very real power on women: the power to name, or to misname, the father. While they are unable to act directly concerning their pregnancies, soap opera women hold the key to family relations and are therefore in a position, however briefly, to define the most important structure in the social world of these shows. Although their control over this structure may be temporary, and is always resolved by incontrovertible biological fact, these women exert a form of power denied to their male counterparts and thus offer the traditional soap opera viewer an opportunity to imagine a world in which women like themselves (i.e., centered on the family) are in control of the central fact of family life.

But this focus on paternity also provides evidence that, however much they may appear to be shaped by women's interests, soap operas are no more radical or woman-centered than any other form of mass-media commercial entertainment. Regardless of the degree of immediate disruption it may cause, the paternity plot always ends with the restoration of family order. In fact, that very restoration demonstrates the strength of the traditional family, presented in soap operas as a structure able to withstand all assaults and to triumph in the face of the greatest threats.[18] Thus, despite the suggestions of critics like Modleski that the active villainesses of soap operas represent a significant departure from traditional portrayals of female passivity, both the constant eruption of the paternity theme and the meaning and prominence given to the inevitable identification of the father continually undermine whatever progressive or woman-centered message we might see in "evil" women shaping the circumstances of their lives. This, then, is the paternity plot's main role in soap operas' vivid restatement of patriarchal ideology.

But that role entails more than the simple repetition of the principle of male dominance. As the typology I outlined in chapter 1 makes clear, viewers must have developed competence in understanding and predicting events on the programs to appreciate fully the intricacies of soap opera plots. In fact, it seems likely that a good deal of viewers' pleasure arises from the recognition that they are superior in knowledge to the shows' characters, a superiority that is especially evident in the presentation of the paternity plot, where regular viewers usually know (or can guess) the father's identity long before the father himself. Given the narrative importance of individual storylines' movement toward closure, this advantageous position is usually crucial to suspense, but at the same time, the very familiarity that aids in building this suspense includes a knowledge of how paternity plots are conventionally resolved. For experienced viewers, then—especially the ones I earlier identified as "competent" and "expert"—the pleasure of watching the mystery unfold must inevitably exist in tension with the realization that it will not remain a mystery for long. And most important for my reading of the paternity plot, that familiarity includes the recognition that whatever family-shaping power the woman has exerted will end when some particular man is finally identified as her baby's father.

It is, of course, profoundly ironic that women viewers should enjoy watching programs that recapitulate what some feminist theorists see as the first stage in women's oppression. As Hilary Radner points out, however, "to say that something is pleasurable for women does not ultimately justify this practice as feminist."[19] The fact that soap operas reenact as fact what in real life could until recently never be more than myth—the absolute identity of the father—makes them a particularly striking example of the way in which popular cultural forms restate and thereby indirectly reinforce the patriarchal status quo. (Perhaps the inevitable reiteration of the father's identity and power also helps to explain the popularity soaps have attained among male viewers.)

But I do not want to suggest that viewing soap operas is simply an exercise in masochism, for there is an important utopian aspect to the repeated reworkings of the paternity plot. I use "utopian" here in the same sense as Janice Radway (who has in turn adopted it from Fredric Jameson), to refer to an "oppositional moment" that permits readers—or in this case, viewers—to participate in a brief fantasy about a more satisfying world.[20] Although many other parts of the viewing experience contribute to women's pleasure in the soaps, I think that the paternity plot itself—or at least that part of it that precedes the final and absolute establishment of paternal identity—constitutes a significant aspect of the enjoyment. The pleasure it produces resides partly in the hope such a plot holds out that women *can* define the family structure, *can* attribute paternity with impunity, *can* name the father according to their own desires and without reference to blood tests. The centrality of the paternity plot also means that, even as the identity of one father is established, viewers can look forward to the eruption of another paternity mystery down the road—another opportunity, however short-lived, for utopian pleasure. If this is so, then the fantasies viewers spin about the shows they watch may be the most radical aspect of them.

However, as Radway repeatedly cautions, while its enjoyment depends on the (often unconscious) recognition of a basic dissatisfaction with things as they are, such a moment of opposition may in fact stand in the way of garnering support for a movement for social change, since it provides a temporary fulfillment of desires unmet in daily life. And the paternity plot's implication in this process goes far beyond its power to distract women from their complaints by offering a fictional substitute for social action. In my view, it is in fact one of the chief methods through which soap operas repress the very resistance women enjoy—not only by incorporating what might be a feminist or protofeminist utopian fantasy into an essentially conservative narrative, but by defusing and ultimately canceling out that fantasy through its inevitable resolution in favor of the father-centered family.

In what has been in part an effort to claim the soap opera as a genre worth taking seriously, feminist critics have tended to argue that its narrative or formal disruptions are sites at which the "feminine" successfully undermines the dominant, or to insist that the serial form and its attention to women's private concerns are themselves inherently progressive. Instead, I would argue that the genre of the soap opera is able simultaneously to vent and to contain those concerns. Laura Mulvey has questioned the common assumption that contradiction automatically undermines ideology, pointing out that "[n]o ideology can even pretend to totality: it must provide an outlet for its own inconsistencies."[21] Her identification of 1950s melodramas as a "safety valve" for the contradictions inherent in the dominant ideology suggests a way of talking about television soap operas.

Mulvey's claim that "[i]deological contradiction is actually the overt mainspring and specific content of melodrama"[22] can, I think, be adapted to soap operas—with an important qualification. In soap operas, contradiction and disruption are raised as content but are then repeatedly smoothed over, resulting in a narrative that maintains rather than undermines the dominant ideology. While these shows allow for the play of women's fantasies—particularly through the workings of the paternity plot—and may therefore provide a pleasurable utopian dream-space, that space is finally both carefully managed and ultimately closed off by the reassertion of the conservative, male-centered ideology the genre promotes.

Questions remain, however, about precisely how the paternity plot has functioned as the genre itself has developed over the last 40 years. Although I have argued that this plot is now a driving force of daytime soap opera narrative, it is not clear when it assumed this dominance, and I am reluctant to speculate very far about whether its current primacy is the result of a unique historical moment or is instead a long-standing feature of the genre. It is, I think, safe to say that the paternity plot, like many other aspects of the soaps and like television in general, has gradually come to involve many more open expressions of sexuality, and this has no doubt multiplied the plotting possibilities. In other words, opportunities for more overt television representations and discussions of sexual behavior have probably expanded soap opera writers' repertoire of paternity plots—permitting them, for instance, to include more stories involving nonmarital relationships, rather than relying (as in the early days of *The Guiding Light*) on husbands who conveniently die shortly after conception. Whether there are, however, more paternity plots now than there were in the 1950s or 1960s has yet to be established.[23]

The importance of this question becomes apparent when we try to think about whether and how soap operas respond to specific changes in the culture at large. For example, it may be that current versions of the paternity plot owe their parameters, and even their origins, to feminist and other challenges to paternal authority. It is tempting to see certain aspects of the paradigm—the intense father-child bond, the reiteration of paternity as the cornerstone of family identity—as responses to specific changes in the family, such as the increasing numbers of female-headed households. Such responses could in turn be interpreted in two diametrically opposed ways: as a demonstration of the dominant ideology's need to make stronger and stronger statements about the primacy of the father during a period of social crisis that threatens to undermine the patriarchal family structure or, conversely, as a dramatic form of wish-fulfillment for women forced to struggle as underpaid single mothers without the safety net of an extended family or adequate social services. In the second case, the paternity plot might serve a nostalgic purpose, comforting women viewers with a memory, however fanciful, of how the now-fragile traditional patriarchal family once solved the problems they currently face.

On the other hand, what looks like a reaction to social shifts may simply be a change in the details by which soap opera writers work out a theme that has actually remained consistent over time. Perhaps the paternity plot only seems to alter because, for example, it is couched in dialogue that uses more direct or more explicit language. Perhaps it simply "reads" differently to an audience that knows about various methods of birth control and hears discussions of abortion on the nightly news, or to viewers who understand the plot, not only on its own terms, but alongside prime-time treatments of sexuality and family. In considering the ideological role of television soap operas, we need to examine not only how they work today, but how they have evolved across the last 40 years, and we must undertake that examination within the context of the evolution of television as a whole.

Still, while there are many questions yet to be asked about the structure of soap operas, the paternity plot remains exemplary of the genre's power to reinforce dominant ideology in a way that viewers continue to find intensely pleasurable. Once again, although critics have focused on the constant interruptions and deferred endings that characterize soap opera narrative, far less attention has been paid either to the ways in which closure is achieved or to the satisfactions that may be provided *between* moments of interruption. If we are to understand the popularity of soap operas—what it is that tempts women to keep watching for years, even for decades—as well as their ideological role, we need to give more thought to the temporary pleasures afforded by plots like those organized around paternity mysteries.

6

Beyond Soap Opera: Ideology, Intertextuality, and the Future of a Television Genre

> Moments of social upheaval and feminist activity have historically produced new variations in the fictional representation of women.
>
> —Resa L. Dudovitz, *The Myth of Superwoman*

> [I]deological production always occurs under contradictory pressures, and . . . its results are therefore never, or rarely, ideologically consistent and uni-dimensional.
>
> —Terry Lovell, "Ideology and *Coronation Street*"

■ I have tried to make a case for the exemplary status of the paternity plot, but it is, of course, only one of the most prominent ways in which soap operas reproduce and reinforce dominant ideology. In fact, implicit and explicit endorsement of male dominance saturates nearly all of the genre's storylines, plot formulas, and individual characterizations. Whether we are talking about the programs' consistent assumption that women's work outside the home is less important or less meaningful than men's, or their representations of women as fulfilled primarily through romantic love and motherhood, or their insistence that feminism is a quasi-pathological affiliation of interest only to villainous or petulant women, it is clear that soap operas do not stray far from the patriarchal status quo.[1]

Yet simply because a program expresses, or appears to express, patriarchal ideology does not mean that regular viewers willingly or uniformly accept that ideology. Nor is such acceptance necessarily required in order for viewers to experience pleasure in the program or genre. Such pleasure may come instead—or additionally—from many other sources: a generic structure that poses complex and multiple narrative enigmas that encourage the audience to engage with the text; a social bond that arises from sharing the viewing experience with friends or coworkers; or simply the opportunity for a restful break in a day filled with domestic and other responsibilities. Indeed, my point throughout this book has been that, for soap fans, pleasures such as these exist in tension with—and at times even in contradiction to—the experience of the genre's ideological imperatives, and I would be remiss if I did not admit that for some viewers, including many of us who identify ourselves as feminists, one of those pleasures involves the very activity of disagreeing with the programs' sexual politics.

Still, the fact that viewers are individually capable of resisting—or simply ignoring—the patriarchal ideology that permeates soap opera does not immediately lessen the genre's role in reproducing and perpetuating that ideology. Nor does it lessen the responsibility of feminist critics and theorists to consider the ways in which the genre participates in the wider network of mass-media expressions, the larger ideological structures whose combined power, redundancy, and relative consistency make resistance more difficult—or, what may be worse, that turn "resistance" into a parlor game in which arguing with the TV set substitutes for participation in movements for social change.

Even more important, perhaps, we need to recognize the extent to which resistance to and enjoyment of particular popular culture artifacts such as soap operas are not mutually exclusive, but simultaneous. Rather than choosing, as David Morley rightly suggests many critics on the left have done, between "optimistic/redemptive readings of mainstream media texts"[2] and an assessment of the mass audience as totally in thrall to, say, the producers of commercial network television, we need to question in a far more sophisticated way how specific groups of viewers come to enjoy popular culture representations that appear to reinforce their subordination.[3] Is it simply a matter of "filter[ing] out that which is negative and select[ing] from the work elements we can relate to"?[4] Or of reading subversively—"against the grain"—in a way that somehow undermines or even reverses the text's apparent ideology? Must we choose between what Morley calls the "implicit valorization of audience pleasure" and the total rejection of pleasure embraced by some feminist and avant-garde theorists?[5]

Or can we finally acknowledge that our pleasure cannot be wholly disentangled from the densely interwoven expressions of capitalist patriarchy that surround us?

As I have suggested throughout this book, one of the greatest challenges facing soap opera theorists is to try to reconcile our conflicting views of the genre, to understand it as somehow unique and at the same time paradigmatic of television forms and practices. In fact, this project of reconciliation is even more complicated than that, for producers and consumers are not the only participants in the struggle over the soap opera text. Although my analysis has until now been primarily textual, I want to turn briefly to an extratextual dimension in order to consider the extent to which the genre's secondary texts, soap opera fan magazines, work to construct yet another kind of viewing experience, one that is different both from that apparently offered by the programs themselves and from those posited by academic theorists.

In what follows, I want to argue that the magazines' emphasis on the apparatus of production in many ways undermines both the narrative strategies of the programs and the efforts of "active" viewers to "read" the soap opera text on their own terms. This construction by part of what Robert Allen has called the "soap opera intertext"[6] involves a collection of specific features that I believe represent *interventions* between the viewer and the soap operas that the magazines attempt to elaborate. As a result, both program producers and magazine editors exert an additional degree of control over the consumption of a television text that theorists usually think of as particularly free of such management.

Soap opera fan magazines originated in the 1970s as home-produced newsletters designed to help women newly employed outside the home keep up with their favorite daytime serials. In their early days, they often resembled other kinds of fan-created materials,[7] but they also represented a new, formalized version of women's traditional networks of "gossip" about the programs.[8] Today, however, the publications have evolved into commercially produced mass-circulation magazines available in grocery, drug, and convenience stores alongside *Time*, *People*, and *TV Guide*. At my local Walgreen's, for instance, I can buy *Soap Opera Weekly*, the biweekly *Soap Opera Digest*, and the occasional *Soap Opera Illustrated*, all published by the K-III Magazine Corp.; *Daytime TV* and its occasional spinoffs, *Daytime Digest*, *Soap Opera Stars*, *Soap Opera Yearbook*, *Daytime TV's Greatest Stories*, *Daytime Super Special*, and *Daytime Soap Opera Special*, published by Sterling/MacFadden Partnership; Bauer Magazine's *Soap Opera Update*; and SOM Publishing, Inc.'s *Soap Opera Magazine*. (And I haven't mentioned more marginal fan-oriented publications, such as the puzzle book *Soap Opera Word-Find*.) In addition, *TV Guide* and major newspapers like the *Chicago Tribune* include weekly soap opera columns that offer plot summaries and gossip/news updates. The commercial TV networks have even begun to participate in this process, producing their own magazines—such as ABC's *Episodes*—and 900-number phone services that provide updates, contests, trivia games, and previews of future story developments. The trend extends to cable (one of E! Entertainment Television's most popular programs was its daily soap update/gossip show, *Pure Soap*) and beyond the United States: Granada Television, the producer of the long-running British serial *Coronation Street*, publishes a companion magazine called *The Street*, which is available by subscription to North American viewers, along with a Canadian fan-produced newsletter.[9]

In *Television Culture*, John Fiske describes commercially produced fan magazines as comprising one of three categories of journalistic writing about TV, locating them between network and studio publicity and what he terms

> independent criticism which seeks to serve the interests of the viewer, either by helping him or her to choose and discriminate, or by provid-

ing a response to a program to confirm or challenge his or hers. Some-where in the middle come the fan magazines that purport to be inde-pendent of the studios, but obviously rely on studio press releases and cooperation for their material and access to the players for interviews.[10]

As that characterization implies, mass-produced soap magazines are far less independent than they appear—or than they were when they first began their lives as fan-created publications. As a matter of fact, their position has been increasingly compromised over the years through the growing participation of the commercial TV broadcast networks for or by whom the serials themselves are produced. The networks have steadily contributed to the magazines' commercial legitimization by providing not just the publicity photos, interview access, and other editorial support that Fiske describes, but direct financial support through the placement of ads for individual shows, and finally, by creating their own versions of the publications. The result is that, rather than existing alongside the programs, the maga-zines have become implicated in the television industry's production of the soap opera text. Circulation numbers suggest, in fact, that the magazines play an important role in the construction of the soap opera viewing experience. The current top two U.S. soaps, CBS's *The Young and the Restless* and ABC's *All My Children*, have audi-ences of about 6.8 million and 5.9 million viewers, respectively. *Soap Opera Digest* reports a circulation of 1.3 million; *Episodes*, about 1 million readers.[11] That means that even in the highly unlikely event that each issue is read by only one person, the top-selling magazines reach at least 20 percent to 30 percent of regular viewers.

The differences between the narrative and programming strate-gies of the producers and networks themselves and the magazines' representations of soaps begin at the most basic level of genre defini-tion, the identification of particular programs as soap operas. The networks categorize soap operas primarily in terms of scheduling: daytime soaps versus prime-time dramas that draw, to a greater or lesser degree, on soap opera conventions. The magazines, on the other hand, define the genre in terms of content, performance style, narra-tive structure, and similar criteria, often ignoring scheduling entirely in order to include specific series in or exclude others from the genre. On the magazines' side, this process of definition clearly contributes to a broader effort of identifying soap opera as a legitimate object both of viewer attention and of professional critics' scrutiny, while the networks mainly attempt to position soaps within their overall broadcasting and advertising agendas.

The networks, for instance, follow the well-established industry policy of identifying programming by broadcast day-part, and promote their daytime soaps separately from nighttime serials and family melodramas. Although promotional spots for daytime programming do sometimes run during prime time, and vice versa—especially when soap performers make prime time appearances—the emphasis tends to be on advertising shows within their own day-parts, and within individual ads, the programs themselves are grouped together according to their place on the schedule. (Similarly, the product advertising that runs during daytime and prime-time shows differs noticeably, with a far higher concentration of housecleaning, laundry, grocery, and baby-care products offered during the day.) In contrast, soap magazines routinely cover prime-time series alongside daytime ones, identifying not just serial-style shows like CBS's *Knots Landing* as soaps, but also narratively conventional ensemble shows like Fox's *Beverly Hills, 90210,* and even traditional, melodramatically inflected series like NBC's (later PBS's) *I'll Fly Away,* which use few of the conventions and virtually nothing of the performance style or production features usually associated with soaps.

This commitment to categorizing programs in terms that go beyond simple scheduling works in reverse as well. The worst condemnation magazine columnists and critics can make of a daytime program they dislike is to say, as *Soap Opera Weekly*'s Marlena De Lacroix did, that "I don't consider [*One Life to Live*] to be a soap opera anymore."[12] More commonly, however, genre definition is inclusive rather than exclusive, relying on an implicit sense of what constitutes a soap opera and paying little regard to producer or network preferences. On occasion, the magazines' editors and in-house critics will openly feud with producers who resist the soap opera label, as the editor of *Soap Opera Weekly* did with the creators of ABC's World War II drama *Homefront*:

> If you were the producer of a struggling TV series in its shaky second season . . . , would you refuse to cooperate with a certain segment of the press, a segment reaching millions of TV viewers, because

doing so would label you a prime-time soap? Wouldn't this be even
more arrogant and foolhardy if you actually were, undeniably, incontrovertibly a prime-time soap. . . ?[13]

(It's worth noting, incidentally, that despite its passion, the editorial
never explains what makes *Homefront* "incontrovertibly" a soap.) The
response of a *Soap Opera Weekly* reader to this diatribe, however, makes
it clear that this is contested terrain:

> As much as we don't like it, the term "soap opera" has a negative
> connotation. Therefore, *Homefront* should have the right to disasso-
> ciate itself from soap publications. And the publications, in return,
> should honor its request graciously.[14]

The magazines' efforts to control the representation of soap opera extend beyond these relatively simple arguments over definition,
however. While they acknowledge characteristics like relatively
nonhierarchical plotting, multiple simultaneous storylines, an emphasis
on long-term story development and suspense, and the incremental
forward movement of individual stories, and even identify them as
crucial in defining the genre, their regular editorial features take an
entirely different stance. The magazines repeatedly undermine the
nonhierarchial character of soap opera narrative, for instance, by emphasizing individual episodes and single "must-see" events. They do
this both prospectively, through weekly or monthly plot summaries,
predictions, and "VCR Alerts," and retrospectively, through their
reconstructions of soap opera history (in, for example, *Soap Opera
Weekly*'s "Flashback" feature, and *Soap Opera Magazine*'s "Remember When" boxes, and through special publications, such as *Soap Opera
Digest*'s 1990 *Looking Back at 60 Years of Soaps*). In fact, the magazines regularly construct a specific hierarchy of stories, evaluating them
in terms of their relative importance to a program's overall narrative
sweep. ("AMC is about Erica," says *Soap Opera Weekly*'s Marlena De
Lacroix, relegating stories that center on other characters to permanent secondary status.)[15] They also arrange the programs themselves
according to relative quality, both through weekly or monthly critical
columns (*Soap Opera Digest*'s "Editor's Choice") and, even more
forcefully, through annual "best" and "worst" features such as *Soap
Opera Magazine*'s "Best Plots of 1992."[16]

Although soaps generate occasional stars such as Susan Lucci, the producers tend to de-emphasize the identities of individual actors—and therefore the power of those actors to disrupt production—by promoting programs or storylines rather than performers, and, even more significantly, by working either to make casting changes invisible or to rationalize them within the program narrative (through such devices as injuries that require extensive cosmetic surgery). In contrast, the magazines construct an elaborate star system through concepts like the "super couple,"[17] the canonization of certain actors as sex symbols,[18] quality ratings like *Soap Opera Digest*'s "Performer of the Week," and through the publication of news and gossip columns about real and speculated casting changes. And their focus extends far beyond big names. Whereas it usually takes the return of a massively popular actor—*All My Children*'s Michael E. Knight, *Days of Our Lives'* Deidre Hall, *General Hospital*'s Tony Geary, and so on—to justify actor-centered on-air or print promotion from the networks themselves, the fan magazines attend to the plans of everyone from bit players to core performers in features like *Soap Opera Weekly*'s "Revolving Door" and *Soap Opera Digest*'s "Comings and Goings" and "Casting About."

The magazines also represent soap performers in a very specific way: as happy, cooperative, hard-working, family-oriented, charity-minded people. The November 3, 1992, issue of *Soap Opera Weekly*, for example, devoted its major feature story to the week's presidential election, beginning with a double-cover picture (continued on the inside cover) in which an assortment of red-, white-, and blue-clad actors posed in front of a huge American flag beneath the titles "We're Voting" and "We're Voting, Too." In the story itself—"Do the Right Thing! Concerned Daytime Stars on Both Coasts Tell Us Why Everyone Should Get Out and Vote Nov. 3"—individual actors were presented as models of civic responsibility as they answered two questions posed by the magazine: "What issue in this election year is most important to you, and what does the right to vote mean to you?" In addition to explaining their positions on specific issues (including abortion, unemployment, and AIDS) and encouraging readers to vote, some performers also endorsed particular candidates.[19]

Soap Opera Digest's "Two of a Kind: Actors Who Are Like Their Characters" took a more typical route to the project of constructing soap actors' personae by profiling a group of soap stars entirely in terms of the traits they shared with their characters.[20] *Guiding Light*'s Vince Williams, for instance, is a musician, much like the character he portrays, while Melissa Reeves is as maternally devoted as her *Days of Our Lives* character Jennifer. Although these shared qualities appear to be coincidental, several of the profiles do mention series writers' deliberate attempts to incorporate aspects of the actors' personalities into their characters. These are, without exception, positive traits: Ruth Warrick's "love of a good time" (p. 102), Jeanne Cooper's "natural sensitivity" (p. 104), and so on. However, lest readers infer from these parallels that actors who play nasty people also share such specific traits with their characters, "Two of a Kind" is accompanied by a sidebar titled "No Way! Actors Who Are Nothing Like Their Characters" (pp. 104-10), which points out that, for instance, *General Hospital* homewrecker Lucy Coe is played by the long-married Lynn Herring, and that Christian LeBlanc is far nicer than the evil lawyer he then portrayed on *The Young and the Restless*.

This kind of sidebar is especially significant because it undermines the claim some critics have made that the magazines' primary strategy is to blur the boundaries between performer and character.[21] In fact, such an editorial tactic really only applies in two kinds of cases: actors who portray consistently good characters, and who are represented in the "Two of a Kind" manner, and actors who have had personal experiences—such as alcoholism or serious illness—that parallel those of the characters they play. A *Soap Opera Weekly* story, "Hope & Glory: Macdonald Carey, Jeanne Cooper, Jess Walton and Nancy Lee Grahn Have Found Strength in Learning to Deal with Addiction," is only one of many, for instance, to emphasize the resemblance between Cooper's alcoholism and that of her *Young and the Restless* character, Katherine Chancellor.[22]

More generally, indeed, rather than eliding differences, the magazines construct a clear distinction between performers and their emotionally turbulent characters by constantly highlighting the actors' happy personal and family lives through interviews, profiles, gossip columns, and coverage of their public appearances. The community of soap opera actors is represented as happy—even gleeful, judging from the frequent pictures of joint birthday parties, vacations, and charity outings—in explicit contrast to the fragmented communities represented by the programs themselves and described just pages away in the magazines' plot summaries. This contrast is emphasized, in fact, through features like *Soap Opera Digest*'s "Bum Raps? Do Some Stars Really Have a Bad Attitude—Or Are They Just Misquoted and Misunderstood?," a story arguing that performers with bad reputations have usually been unfairly confused with the characters they play.[23]

Although this insistence on the distinction between actor and character certainly helps to shape viewer perceptions of how soap operas work, an even more striking difference between the approaches taken by the programs and the magazines concerns their attitudes to the production process itself. While the collaboratively produced programs appear "unauthored"[24] and network promotions pay virtually no attention to writers, directors, technical staff, or other behind-the-scenes personnel, the magazines focus much of their coverage on the distinct features of production and the staff involved in them. Stories, interviews, reviews, and gossip columns consider the contributions of individual members of the production staff, from writers to makeup artists, and emphasize specific aspects of the process of getting a show on the air, from lighting tricks to the costs of specific props and costumes (the last a regular component of *Soap Opera Digest*'s "Did You Know?" column).[25] Like many of the magazines' strategies, attention to the details of production is certainly connected to more general attempts to legitimize the genre in the face of its reputation for poor production values, by showing programs to be the result of complex and highly skilled professional labor.

(Interestingly, this area marks one of the most noticeable differences between a network-produced magazine and an "independent" one, reinforcing the networks' attempts to represent soaps as in some sense "unauthored." Within a month of each other, for example, both ABC's *Episodes* and *Soap Opera Weekly* ran behind-the-scenes photo spreads about *General Hospital*. Of the 13 pictures in the *Soap Opera Weekly* spread, 6 included nonperforming program staff, among them a security guard, makeup artists, the casting director, and the executive producer; of the 15 *Episodes* photos, staff members—the director and the executive producer—were shown in only 2.)[26]

The magazines also elaborate what a friend of mine has called the "soap opera-ization" of the culture at large through soap-themed crossword puzzles and other word games, trivia quizzes, and astrology columns, and, even more forcefully, through such features as *Soap Opera Weekly*'s "Soap Spotting," which cites allusions to soap operas in other media. I would also include in this category *Soap Opera Weekly*'s "Star Track: Life after Soaps," which profiles the current careers of former soap actors, and both its "Moonlighting" stories and "Schedule of Events" listings, which describe performers' upcoming appearances in everything from TV movies to shopping malls. Once again, this is clearly part of the magazines' efforts to identify soaps as significant and worthy of attention by positioning them as culturally pervasive—everyone uses soap operas as a reference point—and by depicting their performers as active in a wide range of professional venues.

Although the programs themselves may offer viewers various kinds of reading opportunities, they do so in a complex and often indirect fashion, in much the same way that all texts provide a range of potential positions for readers/viewers to occupy. Indeed, as I have argued in preceding chapters, soap operas work hard to position viewers, both through specific narrative strategies (story arcs, varying uses of closure, and so on) and through particular ideological messages that coincide with dominant patriarchal expressions. The magazines, on the other hand, create a very specific space for viewers by publishing their letters, columns, polls, and essays—including *Soap Opera Weekly*'s occasional, beautifully titled "Soap Bitch"—and by organizing and covering meetings between viewers and performers. (Although such meetings are often sponsored by magazines and fan groups, however, they take place with the cooperation of the programs themselves, which often require performers to participate in extensive off-camera promotional work.) These efforts go beyond what John Fiske has described as the encouragement of fans' "sense of possession, the idea that stars are constructed by their fans and owe their stardom entirely to them."[27] Despite their acknowledgment of the production apparatus, these magazines openly place fans at the center of the viewing process by providing opportunities for them to express their opinions.[28]

Still, this positioning is not as straightforward as it appears. Earlier in this chapter I called the magazines' various editorial strategies "interventions" between the viewer and the soap operas that are the magazines' subject. I want to return to that characterization now by talking in a little more detail about one of the publications' dominant features. Although some critics have identified the magazines' tactics as "enhanc[ing] the pleasures of the active viewer,"[29] I believe that they actually undermine active "reading" of the programs at the very same time that they seem to enhance it, primarily through their presentation of story previews, program-sanctioned predictions, casting notes, and other information that gives away future storyline developments. Predictions, previews, and "sneak peeks," most provided by the producers themselves, indicate the general direction a story will take. While they are usually brief and often couched in intentionally vague terms, with the details left open until after the week's or month's broadcasts, the difference between a magazine's official publication date and the day it actually appears in the grocery store or mailbox often means that summaries of "past" developments are available before those episodes air. (Readers are occasionally reminded of this fact, as well as of the production apparatus of the shows themselves, when program writers make last-minute script changes that invalidate a published story summary.) Thus, the very features that are meant to keep viewers up-to-date on events they have missed become previews of coming attractions.

But the news and gossip about the comings and goings of individual cast members may be the most powerful intervention these magazines make between viewers and the soap opera text. When a magazine announces, for instance, that a particular actor will be leaving a program and that producers confirm that the part will not be recast, that report immediately limits the possible directions a storyline will take. And when such news includes details about a specific story point, it serves as a kind of plot-summary-before-the-fact that severely limits the kinds of active work in which the viewer can engage.

Let me illustrate with an example of my own experience of this process. Beginning in December, 1992, *All My Children* developed the story of Tad Martin's return to Pine Valley, building suspense about when and how the amnesiac Tad would meet his real family and friends, recover his memory, and choose between his two lives. (For longtime viewers, this story had actually been building off-screen for two years, since the presumably dead Tad was seen getting into a California-bound truck.) Much of the tension centered on wealthy vineyard owner Nola Orsini (played by Barbara Rush), who thought

Tad was her long-lost son Ted, kidnapped in childhood and miraculously restored to her as an adult. To complicate things further, the Pine Valley Tad, whose lineage is even more complicated than that of the average soap opera family member, already had two mothers: his biological mother, Opal Gardner Cortlandt, and his adoptive mother, Ruth Martin. Could he possibly end up with three? Would Nola, hospitalized with a heart condition, stand in the way of Tad's reconciliation with his real family, or accept the inevitable? Would she be able to relinquish her bond with Tad/Ted or would she continue to think of him as her son?

The tension continued to mount until, on January 25, 1993, Nola suddenly began to piece together some of the mystery. At that moment, viewers involved in the story could start to speculate in earnest about exactly how the story would turn out and just what Nola's role in Ted/Tad's eventual rediscovery of his identity would be. Not entirely by chance, however—I was, after all, writing a conference paper about soap opera fan magazines, in which I presented the original version of this analysis—January 25 was also the day I bought the February 2 issue of *Soap Opera Weekly.* While the "Sneak Peeks" entry for the week of the 25th was suitably vague—"Ted loses someone close"[30]—the following notice appeared in the "Revolving Door" column: "OUT: Barbara Rush's last *All My Children* airdate is Jan. 28, when Nola dies" (p. 7). In fact, I actually read the announcement while I was watching that day's episode, and the effect was to point out the precise way the storyline was going to develop: the conflicts between Tad's ties to his real family and his loyalty to Nola would be eliminated by her convenient death, and the only remaining question was exactly when he would be reconciled with them. I even learned that I only had to wait until the end of the week to find out whether Nola would promote, stand in the way of, or miss out entirely on his reconciliation with Opal, Ruth, Dixie, and his other Pine Valley loved ones, and whether she'd leave him her fabulous California estate and multimillion-dollar wine business when she died.[31]

The reaction of another *Soap Opera Weekly* reader makes it clear that the disappointment I experienced is not confined to viewers with an academic interest in soap opera narratives. The week after the Barbara Rush announcement appeared, the magazine printed a letter on a remarkably similar subject:

For weeks since reading that Ellen Marker (Maureen) was leaving [*Guiding Light*], I'd been waiting to find out how she would be written out of the show. Of course, I thought I would get my answer by watching *GL*, so imagine my surprise when I read in Mimi Torchin's editorial that she was being killed. . . .

Torchin's response is illuminating both for its acknowledgment of the importance of viewer anticipation and its implicit assumption that *Weekly* readers consume other fan magazines:

I apologize if I blew the secret. I was under the impression that the fact Maureen was being killed had already been published elsewhere, as we had received several letters from readers who were unhappy about this. I promise I'll be more careful from now on![32]

Little work has been done on soap opera fan magazines and their role in viewers' experience of the genre, but surely their position in the struggle to establish and control the soap opera text is an important one. Speculation about future story developments is, I believe, a major site of active viewers' work as we consume the programs, and when fan magazines provide details like those that revealed Nola's impending death, they exert a particular kind of control over viewers, limiting our options for imagining the narrative's future and cutting off some of our opportunities to engage actively with the text. And what is sometimes even more important, they can spoil the fun of watching soap operas. Charlotte Brunsdon's comment about the pleasures of speculation—"my pleasure . . . is in how my prediction comes true"[33]—describes, I think, the enjoyment that many soap opera viewers experience as we watch our favorite programs. When fan magazines intervene between us, the text is reshaped, the viewing experience itself reconfigured, and much of that pleasure is diminished.[34]

While I have insisted from the beginning on both the possibility and the necessity of defining soap operas as a genre, it is crucial to acknowledge that this is not a rigid or unchanging form. Indeed, my original definition was explicitly designed to be elastic, to allow for the fact that soaps, like all genres, are fluid and shifting—although not, I think, quite as fluid as many theorists have claimed. As we look back over the last 40 years of TV soap operas, we can not only see just how much the genre has changed, but can understand certain specific changes as particularly influential in moving soaps along to their next stages of development. Among the more important production-centered shifts, for example, we might identify the gradual expansion to a one-hour format, which led to the inclusion of more (and more complicated) storylines; the introduction of outdoor locations, which added an air of realism and intensified the sense of the shows' connection to the outside world; and the increasingly overt portrayal of sexuality, which subtly shifted the programs' visual and narrative economies.

I would still argue that the traits I identified in chapter 2—fictionality, interlocking storylines, multiple weekly episodes, serial presentation, a focus on relationships within a community—remain the defining frame of the genre, but new features continue to emerge. It is far too early, of course, to guess where the latest changes will lead, or exactly which ones will turn out in retrospect to have been most influential in altering the genre's basic parameters. It is also easy to be completely mistaken about just how important certain changes will be. For example, for many years critics predicted that the thorough integration of African American characters into the soap community and, most significantly, into the romance and kinship circles that form its basis, would fundamentally alter that community.[35] Now that such integration has finally taken place, however, with mixed-race couples established on *All My Children*, *General Hospital*, *One Life to Live*, and *As the World Turns*, it has become apparent that the simple presence of African Americans in core families and long-term story arcs does not change the rules of the genre, but merely draws members of previously excluded groups into the shows' existing communities.

Still, it is tempting to try to imagine what other changes would actually have the kind of impact many expected from televisual racial equality. Among those imaginary possibilities, the full integration of openly gay and lesbian characters seems to have some of the greatest potential power to disrupt the traditional soap ethos, because the long-term presence of such characters in the soap opera community would necessarily undermine the shows' basic (heterosexually centered) conceptions of love, romance, and family. What, for instance, would happen to the programs' emphasis on kinship and to staples like the paternity plot if "family" was redefined—as it would necessarily be with the introduction of gay or lesbian partnerships—to mean something beyond ties of blood and law? Yet, as was the case with ethnic minorities, this kind of disruption will require far more than the mere presence of an openly gay or lesbian character. If *One Life to Live*'s 1992 homophobia/AIDS story arc proved anything, it was that soaps can develop an extremely high-profile drama involving gay identity that remains completely consistent with the genre's traditions and that never seriously strains its conceptions of sexuality or community. At least two things now seem clear: Gay and lesbian characters will have to be maintained as a visible, long-term presence on the shows before they can be taken seriously as full members of the community; and the genre's conceptions of family, sexuality, community, and so on must be challenged through story arcs that directly engage the threat that such characters represent.

However, when we consider both the integration of African American characters into the shows' most basic romantic and kinship circles and the *One Life to Live* homophobia arc, what looks like failure can from a different angle be seen as good news. After all, these developments prove that potentially disruptive figures *can* be introduced into the soap opera community without causing it to disintegrate, and while that testifies to the strength of the genre's ideological constraints, it also suggests just how elastic the form actually is when it comes to certain kinds of ideological expressions. If Pine Valley and Port Charles can each accommodate mixed-race families and Llanview can provide a home for a gay teen, isn't it possible to imagine a Genoa City woman choosing an abortion without suffering horrific recriminations, or a Bay City man supporting his wife's choice of work over motherhood without wishing she was a "real woman"?[36]

One recent development in soap opera storytelling also seems to have the potential to alter the genre's most basic narrative structures, and to hint at some of the directions in which it may develop in the near future: the creation of crossover storylines between programs and of characters who move from one soap to another. This is not a completely new trend, for characters and locations from one program have had occasional and limited functions on others since the 1960s. There has long been a tie, for instance, between *All My Children*'s Pine Valley and *One Life to Live*'s Llanview, which are supposed to be located within driving distance of each other, and characters have from time to time shared the same doctors, shopped at the same stores, visited the same nearby towns, and even read the same tabloid scandal sheet. In a few cases, major characters from these and other programs have made intranetwork visits to other shows, but beyond two attempts to create spinoffs from NBC's *Another World* (*Another World—Somerset* in 1970 and *Texas* in 1980), these exchanges have rarely played a significant part in story development. Instead, they have more closely resembled the Christmas, wedding, and funeral appearances of long-gone characters, serving as suggestions—but little more than suggestions—that the fictional communities in question exist as part of a larger world, and that characters who leave town do not fall off the edge of the earth.

This changed, however, in the early 1990s, when several soaps merged their fictional worlds in a far more profound and potentially significant way. On ABC, characters visited back and forth between *Loving*'s Corinth and *All My Children*'s Pine Valley, where the Corinthians eventually became embroiled in a front-burner domestic-abuse storyline that went on for some months. Soon after this story's resolution, two major Pine Valley characters, Ceara and Jeremy Hunter, moved to Corinth, where Ceara was killed in an airport shootout. But Jeremy's move was permanent: He (and the actor who played him) was fully absorbed into the Corinth community and rapidly became involved in prominent storylines.

An even more elaborate merger occurred on CBS, where *The Young and the Restless* villainess Sheila Grainger, apparently killed in a fire, showed up the next week on *The Bold and the Beautiful*. Like the *All My Children/Loving* crossovers, this event was a far cry from earlier attempts to cash in on the popularity of a departed character by casting the same actor in a similar role on another program, for in both cases—and most strikingly on CBS—characters were not only transplanted intact from one show to another, but continued the storylines they had originally been in. In the case of the CBS soaps, in fact, the story of the rivalry between Sheila and her *Young and the Restless* nemesis Lauren Fenmore (rooted, interestingly enough, in an elaborate combination paternity-maternity plot) was played out over the next year in episodes on both serials, with Sheila visiting her mother on *The Young and the Restless* and both Lauren and her ex-lover Brad Carlton eventually pursuing Sheila to *The Bold and the Beautiful*.[37]

Since those stories developed, ABC has transplanted still more people from one soap to another, reviving characters who had left series some years ago and placing them on new programs, with the same actors appearing in their original roles. *One Life to Live*'s comic con man Marco Dane, for example, relocated to *General Hospital*'s Port Charles, while *General Hospital*'s mysterious villain Cesar Faison turned up on *Loving*—chasing the newly transplanted Jeremy Hunter!—and *All My Children*'s Angie Hubbard became *Loving*'s newest doctor. (In 1993, as if to reinforce the importance of this trend, Gerald Anthony, who created the role of Marco Dane, became the first actor ever to get daytime Emmy awards for playing the same part on two different shows.)[38]

The crossovers between *Loving* and *All My Children* and between *The Young and the Restless* and *The Bold and the Beautiful* began as ratings strategies designed to draw viewers of the networks'—indeed, the genre's—most popular soaps into the fictional orbits of their least-watched ones. Prime-time series have long used the same strategy of having characters from one show "visit" another, often a fictionally unrelated one, and ABC's *Roseanne* carried this to a new extreme of cross-fertilization during the 1993-94 season with visits by characters from both *General Hospital* and *One Life to Live*, while Roseanne and Tom Arnold appeared in small parts on *General Hospital*.[39] Yet the ongoing relocation of characters to new soaps suggests that this has become something more than a mere gimmick. If it continues to be a feature of soap opera narrative, the long-term impact could be enormous, disrupting the genre's narrative structure by undermining long-standing ideas about what constitutes the soap opera community. Despite increasing efforts to locate them within broader fictional and nonfictional worlds, the communities themselves have always been depicted as small, closed, and to a great extent separate from the larger world inhabited by viewers. Even when soaps take place in real cities, as in the case of *Ryan's Hope* (New York City), *Generations* (Chicago), *Capitol*, and *Santa Barbara*, the programs themselves have focused on small communities within those cities— made up, as I demonstrated in chapter 3, of an intimately connected network of families, friends, enemies, and neighbors. By setting up connections *between* those small groups, however, the crossover soaps hint that the boundaries of their communities may be far more flexible than the genre has previously admitted. It even seems possible that the communities themselves could eventually stretch far past their present limits, moving beyond the densely entwined bonds that permit the constant interference I have identified as the power behind the genre's main storylines. The expansion of the soap opera community in a way that takes seriously the *non*intimate ties that characterize real-world community life would, I think, lead to—indeed, demand—a fundamental shift in the programs' narratives.

The existence of crossover stories also raises questions about the concept of the soap opera text itself. Many critics and theorists have, as I have noted, contested the very idea of identifying something called "the" soap opera text, and while I would still like to hold out for the possibility, surely the development of crossover storylines makes it an even more complicated task. If characters can travel regularly from one soap to another, expanding the idea of what constitutes a community, their movements also force us to ponder exactly what constitutes a soap opera and where its limits lie. Could *The Bold and the Beautiful* and *The Young and the Restless* be incorporated even more closely, with additional characters becoming simultaneously entangled in stories on both shows? If characters who have left one show continue to turn up on another, will *Loving, All My Children, One Life to Live*, and *General Hospital* ultimately merge into a single gigantic ABC mega-soap?[40]

And if these changes occur, what might their impact be on our conceptions of the TV programming that surrounds the soaps? Surely there would be far-reaching effects beyond those implied by the contention that soap opera is paradigmatic of TV as a whole. Currently, discussions of the future of television programming tend to emphasize interactive "information highway" systems and other high-tech developments, focusing primarily on viewers' increasing potential participation in the actual creation of shows (through, say, the selection of story resolutions), and on the ways in which TV might be made to serve nonentertainment purposes (shopping, voting, banking). Less attention has been paid to how industry-created programming might be radically altered from the production side, but soap opera crossover stories should remind us of the potential power of such shifts, the effect of changes that could eventually make the notion of the "televisual supertext" far more than just a useful metaphor.[41]

Yet whatever changes take place in either the genre or the larger televisual landscape, the relationship between soap opera viewer and text will likely continue to be organized around the same point of tension that anchors it today. Because viewer expertise consists of a sophisticated knowledge of both specific and generic narrative strategies, story formulas, and performance and production practices, the pleasure of watching involves simultaneously predicting and hoping to be wrong about what will happen next. As we watch *All My Children* or *Guiding Light*, using our years of viewing experience to guess exactly what the next development will be, we also fantasize that the program will surprise us by suddenly turning a long-standing convention on its head, or taking a familiar storyline in a dramatic new direction. Whether or not we are feminist viewers, our fantasies about those new twists draw on our dissatisfaction with the way things are, and may even help us to imagine fictional solutions to the problems women face in the real world. We need to remember, however, that pleasure is not the only thing at stake in our consumption of soaps, for the genre of soap opera and the individual programs that comprise it help to promote and maintain patriarchal ideology in very specific ways, undermining our most utopian plot-fantasies at the very moment we conceive them. It will take more than our individual imaginations to change that.

NOTES

1. Viewing Histories and Textual Difficulties

1. Brad Chisholm, "Difficult Viewing: The Pleasures of Complex Screen Narratives," *Critical Studies in Mass Communication* 8, no. 4 (December 1991): 391.

2. Elspeth Probyn, *Sexing the Self: Gendered Positions in Cultural Studies* (London: Routledge, 1993), pp. 23–25.

3. Carol Traynor Williams offers a particularly harsh view of this tendency in *"It's Time for My Story": Soap Opera Sources, Structure, and Response* (Westport, CT: Praeger, 1992), pp. 7–11. Jim Collins considers the broader theoretical issues implicated in the way intellectuals position themselves as both viewers and critics/theorists in "Watching Ourselves Watch Television, or Who's Your Agent?", *Cultural Studies* 3, no. 3 (October 1989): 261–81. For an analysis of some of these questions at the intersections of gender, sexuality, and cultural studies—and one that is in many ways a critique of my own use of personal experience in this chapter—see Probyn, *Sexing the Self.*

4. Charlotte Brunsdon, "*Crossroads*: Notes on Soap Opera," in *Regarding Television: Critical Approaches—An Anthology*, ed. E. Ann Kaplan (Los Angeles: American Film Institute/University Publications of America, 1983), p. 81.

5. Cf. Ellen Seiter's reference, in "Eco's TV Guide—The Soaps," *Tabloid*, no. 5 (Winter 1982), to the "encyclopaedic competence" of the "experienced viewer," who is "encouraged to relate a given scene to this intertextual knowledge and interpret it accordingly" (p. 38).

6. See David Morley, *Television, Audiences and Cultural Studies* (London: Routledge, 1992), pp. 29–30, 128–29; Seiter, "Eco's TV Guide"; and Robert C. Allen, *Speaking of Soap Operas* (Chapel Hill: University of North Carolina Press, 1985), pp. 81–84.

7. Stuart Hall, "Encoding/decoding," in *Culture, Media, Language: Working Papers in Cultural Studies, 1972–79*, ed. Stuart Hall, Dorothy Hobson, Andrew Lowe, and Paul Willis (London: Hutchinson, 1980), p. 138. Jim Collins has suggested that today, even mainstream viewers perform a complicated, ironic, and ambivalent reading that combines a traditional straightforward acceptance of the dominant message with the distantiation commonly granted to subcultural viewers; see "Watching Ourselves Watch Television," pp. 271–73.

8. Charlotte Brunsdon, "Text and Audience," in *Remote Control: Television, Audiences and Cultural Power*, ed. Ellen Seiter, Hans Borchers, Gabriele

Kreutzner, and Eva-Maria Warth (London: Routledge, 1989), p. 125. See also Brunsdon's "Television: Aesthetics and Audiences," in *Logics of Television*, ed. Patricia Mellencamp (Bloomington: Indiana University Press, 1990), pp. 59–72; and John Hartley's even more definitive assertion that he is "an avowed textualist," *Tele-ology: Studies in Television* (London: Routledge, 1992), p. 119.

9. Chisholm, "Difficult Viewing," p. 401.

10. Christine Gledhill, "Pleasurable Negotiations," in *Female Spectators: Looking at Film and Television*, ed. E. Deidre Pribram (London: Verso, 1988), p. 74. See also Morley, *Television, Audiences and Cultural Studies*, pp. 18–41, especially his critique of the strand of cultural studies shaped by John Fiske's work, pp. 26–32.

11. See, among others, Jane Feuer, "The Concept of Live Television: Ontology as Ideology," in Kaplan, *Regarding Television*, pp. 12–22; Stuart Hall and John O'Hara, "The Narrative Construction of Reality: An Interview with Stuart Hall," *Southern Review* 17, no. 1 (March 1984): 3–17; and David Barker, "'It's Been Real': Forms of Television Representation," *Critical Studies in Mass Communication* 5, no. 1 (March 1988): 42–56.

12. The germinal presentation of this argument is of course Laura Mulvey, "Visual Pleasure and Narrative Cinema," *Screen* 16, no. 3 (Autumn 1975): 6–18. Among the many responses to and revisions of Mulvey's work, see Annette Kuhn, "Women's Genres: Melodrama, Soap Opera and Theory," *Screen* 25, no. 1 (1984): 18–28; and Gledhill, "Pleasurable Negotiations."

13. Discussions of the concept of ideology are so numerous, and my view of its workings draws on so many different theories, that it is difficult to cite one or two, even as representatives of influential ideas. For a useful overview of the concept as it relates specifically to television, see Mimi White, "Ideological Analysis and Television," in *Channels of Discourse, Reassembled: Television and Contemporary Criticism*, 2nd ed., ed. Robert C. Allen (Chapel Hill: University of North Carolina Press, 1992), pp. 161–202.

14. Once again, discussions of the term "patriarchy" have been lengthy and complicated, and I have been influenced by a wide variety of views. A typical critique of uses like my own comes from Jane Gaines:

> When we have foregrounded one antagonism in our analysis, we have misunderstood another, and this is most dramatically illustrated in the applications of the notion of patriarchy. Feminists have not been absolutely certain what they mean by patriarchy . . . but what is consistent about the use of the concept is the rigidity of the structure it describes . . . as in the radical feminist theory of patriarchal order which sees oppression in all forms and through all ages as derived from the male/female division. . . . Unfortunately, this deterministic model . . . [leaves] us with no sense of movement, or no idea of how women have acted to change their condition. . . . [And] is most obtuse when it disregards the position white women occupy over Black men as well as Black women.

"White Privilege and Looking Relations: Race and Gender in Feminist Film Theory," in *Issues in Feminist Film Criticism*, ed. Patricia Erens (Bloomington: Indiana University Press, 1990), p. 202.

15. One of the earliest and most influential feminist uses of this term is Zillah R. Eisenstein, "Developing a Theory of Capitalist Patriarchy and Socialist Feminism," in her *Capitalist Patriarchy and the Case for Socialist Feminism* (New York: Monthly Review Press, 1979), pp. 5–40.

2. What Is This Thing Called Soap Opera?

1. For example, Mary Ellen Brown lists the following as general characteristics of the genre:

1. serial form which resists narrative closure;
2. multiple characters and plots;
3. use of time which parallels actual time and implies that the action continues to take place whether we watch it or not;
4. abrupt segmentation between parts;
5. emphasis on dialogue, problem solving, and intimate conversation;
6. many of the male characters portrayed as "sensitive men";
7. female characters often professional or otherwise powerful in the world outside the home;
8. the home, or some other place which functions as a home, is the setting for the show.

See "The Politics of Soaps: Pleasure and Female Empowerment," *Australian Journal of Cultural Studies* 4, no. 2 (1987): 4.

2. Ellen Seiter, Hans Borchers, Gabriele Kreutzner, and Eva-Maria Warth, "'Don't Treat Us Like We're So Stupid and Naive': Toward an Ethnography of Soap Opera Viewers," in *Remote Control: Television, Audiences and Cultural Power*, ed. Ellen Seiter, Hans Borchers, Gabriele Kreutzner, and Eva-Maria Warth (London: Routledge, 1989), p. 234.

3. Charlotte Brunsdon, "Text and Audience," in Seiter et al., *Remote Control*, p. 123.

4. Robert C. Allen, *Speaking of Soap Operas* (Chapel Hill: University of North Carolina Press, 1975), p. 3. Social scientists like Muriel G. Cantor and Suzanne Pingree may add more details, but they still describe soap opera as "a form of serialized dramatic television broadcast daily over the three commercial television networks . . . usually during the afternoon," *The Soap Opera* (Beverly Hills: Sage Publications, 1983), p. 19. Even a guide for would-be scriptwriters, Jean Rouverol's *Writing for the Soaps* (Cincinnati: Writer's Digest Books, 1984), never actually defines soap operas, but assumes its readers' familiarity with the genre and its conventions, and offers instructions on the production process and hints about how to break into the business. Among the other writers who have specifically tried to define the form is Christine Geraghty, "The Continuous Serial—A Definition," in *Coronation Street*, ed. Richard Dyer, Christine Geraghty, Marion Jordan, Terry Lovell, Richard Paterson, and John Stewart (London: British Film Institute, 1981), pp. 9–26. While her essay contains many important observations about the serial structure, however, Geraghty explicitly confines her discussion to British pro-

grams. Other recent attempts to define the genre within a U.S. context include Martha Nochimson, *No End to Her: Soap Opera and the Female Subject* (Berkeley: University of California Press, 1992) and Carol Traynor Williams, *"It's Time for My Story": Soap Opera Sources, Structure, and Response* (Westport, CT: Praeger, 1992), especially pp. 61–70. For a brief review of other critical attempts to define the genre, see Robert C. Allen, "Bursting Bubbles: 'Soap Opera,' Audiences, and the Limits of Genre," in Seiter et al., *Remote Control*, pp. 44–55.

5. Among examples from the popular media, *Twin Peaks* has been called a "soap noir" (*New York Times*, May 5, 1991, section 2, p. 1) and a "prime-time soap" (*Entertainment Weekly*, no. 8 [April 6, 1990]: 6). In his book *Three Blind Mice: How the TV Networks Lost Their Way* (New York: Random House, 1991), Ken Auletta groups *Dynasty* and *Hotel* together as "prime-time soap operas" (p. 45). *TV Guide*, which runs a weekly page of soap opera plot summaries confined entirely to daytime serials, is less precise on other pages, calling the ensemble drama *Homefront*, for instance, "ABC's post-WWII soap" (July 18, 1992, p. 2), and *Soap Opera Weekly*'s editor, Mimi Torchin, devoted her November 11, 1992, column to her conflict with *Homefront*'s producers over the series' status as a soap opera (p. 4). Fan magazines regularly blur genre boundaries by including prime-time programs, from *Knots Landing* to the revived *Dark Shadows* and *Twin Peaks*, in their plot summaries and treating actors from those series as part of the community of soap performers. *Soap Opera Digest*'s special issue, *Looking Back At: 60 Years of Soaps* (Winter 1991) featured a "comprehensive" list of TV soaps that included not only the predictable prime-time serials, but the public television broadcasts of *The Forsyte Saga* and *Upstairs, Downstairs* as well. In *From Mary Noble to Mary Hartman: The Complete Soap Opera Book* (New York: Stein and Day, 1976), Madeleine Edmondson and David Rounds document the fan-magazine debate over the correct genre categorization of *Mary Hartman, Mary Hartman*, pp. 173–85.

Among scholars, the subtitle to Ien Ang's book *Watching Dallas: Soap Opera and the Melodramatic Imagination*, trans. Della Couling (London: Methuen, 1985) is only one of many such references. Lidia Curti, who includes both *Dallas* and *Dynasty* in the category, has gone so far as the formulation, "Women's television, that is, soap opera"; see "What Is Real and What Is Not: Female Fabulations in Cultural Analysis," in *Cultural Studies*, ed. Lawrence Grossberg, Cary Nelson, and Paula Treichler (Champaign: University of Illinois Press, 1992), p. 142.

6. Cantor and Pingree, *The Soap Opera*, p. 26; Ang, *Watching Dallas*, p. 55. Despite her disclaimers, however, Ang's usage throughout the book indicates that she considers *Dallas* and programs like it to be soap operas of some kind.

7. Jane Feuer, for example, stresses "the similarities between daytime soaps and the prime-time continuing melodramatic serials," arguing that they "share a narrative form . . . [and] concentrate on the domestic sphere," "Melodrama, Serial Form and Television Today," *Screen* 25, no. 1 (January–February 1984): 4.

8. Gabriele Kreutzner and Ellen Seiter, "Not All 'Soaps' Are Created Equal: Towards a Crosscultural Criticism of Television Serials," *Screen* 32,

no. 2 (Summer 1991): 156. See also Feuer, "Melodrama, Serial Form and Television Today," p. 5.

9. Christine Geraghty, *Women and Soap Opera: A Study of Prime Time Soaps* (Cambridge: Polity Press, 1991), p. 4.

10. Geraghty, *Women and Soap Opera*, p. 5.

11. Lynn Spigel discusses this phenomenon throughout *Make Room for TV: Television and the Family Ideal in Postwar America* (Chicago: University of Chicago Press, 1992), e.g., pp. 113, 116–18, 139. See also Laura Mulvey, "Melodrama Inside and Outside the Home," in her *Visual and Other Pleasures* (Bloomington: Indiana University Press, 1989), pp. 63–77.

12. For a suggestion of the breadth of work done under the banner of cultural studies and the ways that individual viewers attempt to make personal meanings out of mass-produced media products, see Grossberg et al., *Cultural Studies*, especially the essays by Rosalind Brunt, Lidia Curti, John Fiske, and Constance Penley.

13. See Gloria-Jean Masciarotte, "C'mon Girl: Oprah Winfrey and the Discourse of Feminine Talk," *Genders* 11 (Fall 1991): 81–110.

14. Geraghty, *Women and Soap Opera*, p. 3.

15. Mimi White, "Television Genres: Intertextuality," *Journal of Film and Video* 37, no. 3 (Summer 1985): 41.

16. Jane Feuer, "Narrative Form in American Network Television," in *High Theory/Low Culture: Analysing Popular Television*, ed. Colin MacCabe (New York: St. Martin's Press, 1986), p. 111. Among discussions of the genre mixing that seems increasingly to characterize television, see White, "Television Genres," and Todd Gitlin's discussion of "recombinant" TV in *Inside Prime Time* (New York: Pantheon Books, 1983), pp. 77–81.

17. See for instance E. Ann Kaplan, *Rocking around the Clock: Music Television, Postmodernism, and Consumer Culture* (New York: Methuen, 1987), esp. pp. 143–53; and her edited collection, *Postmodernism and Its Discontents: Theories, Practices* (London: Verso, 1988).

18. John Fiske, *Television Culture* (London: Methuen, 1987), p. 112.

19. John Caughie, "Adorno's Reproach: Repetition, Difference and Television Genre," *Screen* 32, no. 2 (Summer 1991): 128.

20. See Thomas Schatz, *Hollywood Genres: Formulas, Filmmaking, and the Studio System* (Philadelphia: Temple University Press, 1981), p. 6.

21. Cf. John Caughie's remark in "Adorno's Reproach" that, "With *Twin Peaks*, the fascination is in watching, with mounting incredulity, the parodic games of multiple genres and thoroughly cliched conventions" (p. 149); and Jim Collins's discussion of *Twin Peaks* as an example of the "policing" of the boundaries between "high" and "low" art in "Television and Postmodernism," in *Channels of Discourse, Reassembled: Television and Contemporary Criticism*, 2nd. ed., ed. Robert C. Allen (Chapel Hill: University of North Carolina Press, 1992), pp. 341–49. See also Richard Dienst's discussion of *Twin Peaks*, in *Still Life in Real Time: Theory after Television* (Durham: Duke University Press, 1994), pp. 89–99.

22. Caughie, "Adorno's Reproach," p. 149.

23. Patricia Mellencamp, *High Anxiety: Catastrophe, Scandal, Age, & Comedy* (Bloomington: Indiana University Press, 1990), p. 240.

24. Caughie, "Adorno's Reproach," p. 127. See for example Fiske, *Tele-*

vision Culture, pp. 109–15; John Tulloch, *Television Drama: Agency, Audience and Myth* (London: Routledge, 1990), pp. 58–86; and Jane Feuer, "Genre Study," in Allen, *Channels of Discourse, Reassembled*, pp. 138–60.

25. Among the earliest theoretical explorations of this difference is Stephen Heath and Gillian Skirrow, "Television: A World in Action," *Screen* 18, no. 2 (Summer 1977): 7–59.

26. Feuer, "Narrative Form in American Network Television," p. 101.

27. David Thorburn, "Television Melodrama," in *Television: The Critical View*, 4th ed., ed. Horace Newcomb (New York: Oxford University Press, 1987), p. 631.

28. Mulvey, "Melodrama Inside and Outside the Home," p. 65. See also Peter Brooks, *The Melodramatic Imagination: Balzac, Henry James, Melodrama, and the Mode of Excess* (New Haven: Yale University Press, 1976).

29. Mulvey, "Melodrama Inside and Outside the Home," p. 76.

30. Lynne Joyrich, "All That Television Allows: TV Melodrama, Postmodernism and Consumer Culture," *Camera Obscura*, no. 16 (1988): 130; subsequent references cited in text.

31. See Thomas Schatz's discussion of the family melodrama in *Hollywood Genres*, pp. 221–60.

32. Robyn Wiegman, "Melodrama, Masculinity, and the Televisual War," paper presented at the first annual conference, Console-ing Passions: Television, Video, and Feminism, April 1992, Iowa City, Iowa, p. 7. See also Caren J. Deming's discussion of TV melodrama in "For Television-Centred Television Criticism: Lessons from Feminism," in *Television and Women's Culture: The Politics of the Popular*, ed. Mary Ellen Brown (London: Sage Publications, 1990), pp. 53–58.

33. Christine Gledhill, "Speculations on the Relationship between Soap Opera and Melodrama," *Quarterly Review of Film and Video* 14, no. 1–2 (1992): 103–24; subsequent references cited in text. See also her statement in the introduction to *Home Is Where the Heart Is: Studies in Melodrama and the Women's Film* (London: British Film Institute, 1987) that "soap opera is commonly seen as the last resort of melodrama. But soap opera, like the woman's film, has an affiliation with women's culture, the elision of which with melodrama should not be assumed" (p. 2).

34. Wiegman, "Melodrama, Masculinity, and the Televisual War," p. 8.

35. Brunsdon, "Text and Audience," p. 119; subsequent references cited in text. See also her "Problems with Quality," *Screen* 31, no. 1 (Spring 1990): 67–90.

36. Jerry Palmer, *Potboilers: Methods, Concepts and Case Studies in Popular Fiction* (London: Routledge, 1991), p. 7.

37. Allen, *Speaking of Soap Operas*, p. 14.

38. Robert C. Allen, "On Reading Soaps: A Semiotic Primer," in *Regarding Television: Critical Perspectives—An Anthology*, ed. E. Ann Kaplan (Los Angeles: University Publications of America/American Film Institute, 1983), p. 98. See also Dennis Porter, "Soap Time: Thoughts on a Commodity Art Form," *College English* 38, no. 8 (April 1977): 782–88, especially his claim that a soap opera's "beginnings are always lost sight of" (p. 783).

39. John Caughie contends that television actually continues the tradition of "novelistic" discourse that film, with its single-sitting pattern of consumption, interrupts, "Adorno's Reproach," p. 141.

40. Heath and Skirrow, "Television," p. 54. For the original conception of television's "flow," see Raymond Williams, *Television: Technology and Cultural Form* (New York: Schocken Books, 1975), pp. 86–96.

41. Feuer, "The Concept of Live Television," p. 19; subsequent references cited in text.

42. See Geraghty, "The Continuous Serial," p. 10; and Dorothy Hobson, *"Crossroads": The Drama of a Soap Opera* (London: Methuen, 1982), pp. 34–35. Examples of the coincidence between characters' and viewers' time include the soaps' regular celebration of holidays and their frequent allusions to actual days of the week or month. Soap time does not, however, pass in a consistent manner, but is manipulated for diegetic purposes. The classic example of this practice is the aging of child characters, who may pass miraculously from infancy to adolescence to adulthood. Some writers have identified the passage of time on soap operas as itself a basic feature of the genre. For example, in *The Soap Opera*, Muriel Cantor and Suzanne Pingree call the programs' pace "very slow" (p. 23) and explicitly contrast the rate of story development with the "much more rapid" pace of the prime-time *Peyton Place* (p. 27).

43. Porter, "Soap Time," p. 783.

44. Seiter et al., "'Don't Treat Us Like We're So Stupid and Naive,'" p. 233; subsequent references cited in text.

45. Robert C. Allen, "Bursting Bubbles," p. 45. See also Jane Feuer's position that, at least in the case of *Dynasty*, "the reading formation *is* the text," "Reading *Dynasty*: Television and Reception Theory," *SAQ* 88, no. 2 (Spring 1989): 458.

46. Steve Neale, "Questions of Genre," *Screen* 31, no. 1 (Spring 1990): 46, 56.

47. See Brown, "The Politics of Soaps"; Seiter et al., "'Don't Treat Us Like We're So Stupid and Naive'"; and Elihu Katz and Tamar Liebes, "Decoding *Dallas*: Notes from a Cross-Cultural Study," in Newcomb, *Television*, pp. 419–32.

48. Some critics have closely interrogated the deployment of the term "soap opera," pointing out the ways in which it has come to be associated with commercialism (versus "real" art), low quality, and even to stand for U.S. television and culture. In "Text and Audience," for instance, Charlotte Brunsdon calls this "a little connotational string: soap opera—television—commercial—American" (p. 117).

49. Stephen Neale, *Genre* (London: British Film Institute, 1980), pp. 22–23.

50. Although their humor obviously depends on at least some knowledge of the original, the fact that parodies can be appreciated even by viewers with relatively little experience of soap operas demonstrates how far knowledge of the genre's conventions pervades the culture. The general outlines of the form are so widely recognized that written parodies may appear in publications that cannot necessarily assume their readers' familiarity with specific soap operas. One example is Ian Frazier, "Have You Ever," *The New Yorker* 68, no. 1 (February 24, 1992): 34–35.

51. Feuer, "Reading *Dynasty*," pp. 447, 456; and "Melodrama, Serial Form and Television Today," p. 9. See also Caughie, "Adorno's Reproach," pp. 150–53.

52. Tania Modleski, *Loving with a Vengeance: Mass-Produced Fantasies for Women* (New York: Methuen, 1984), pp. 85–109.

53. Charlotte Brunsdon, "*Crossroads*: Notes on Soap Opera," in Kaplan, *Regarding Television*, pp. 76–83.

54. Modleski, for instance, argues that "soap opera stimulates women's desire for connectedness . . . through the constant, claustrophobic use of close-up shots," *Loving with a Vengeance*, p. 99.

55. Tulloch, *Television Drama*, p. 211.

56. Seiter et al., "'Don't Treat Us Like We're So Stupid and Naive,'" pp. 230–31. There is also evidence that some of these viewers think of the time they spend watching soap operas as a regular respite from their responsibilities in the home. Cf. Janice A. Radway's description of Gothic romance readers in *Reading the Romance: Women, Patriarchy and Popular Literature* (Chapel Hill: University of North Carolina Press, 1984), pp. 86–118.

57. Feuer, "The Concept of Live Television," p. 19. See also John Ellis's contention that "the intimacy that broadcast TV sets up is . . . made qualitatively different by the sense that the TV image carries of being a live event," *Visible Fictions: Cinema, Television, Video*, rev. ed. (London: Routledge, 1989), p. 136.

58. Brunsdon, "Text and Audience," p. 125. Cf. Andrew Ross's distinction between "*everyday* life . . . [and] *everyweek* life. For most people there is no such thing as everyday life, but rather weekly cycles of work and leisure, both in and out of the home," "All in the Family: On David Morley's *Family Television: Cultural Power and Domestic Leisure* and Philip Simpson's (ed.) *Parents Talking Television*," *Camera Obscura*, no. 16 (January 1988): 169.

59. Caughie, "Adorno's Reproach," p. 141.

60. Caughie, "Adorno's Reproach," p. 145. In the context of the soaps themselves, cf. Martha Nochimson's contention that "the dailiness of the gap [between episodes] insures a less hierarchical, less linear relationship among story lines," *No End to Her*, p. 35.

61. Heath and Skirrow, "Television," p. 15. See also Williams, *Television*, pp. 89–96; and Tulloch's claim that "television drama texts are defined as much by the regime of watching as by their conditions of performance, production and circulation, and have effect as part of the domestic routine," *Television Drama*, p. 228.

62. Dorothy Hobson discusses this same issue in *Crossroads*, pp. 26–32.

63. Sean Cubitt, *Timeshift: On Video Culture* (London: Routledge, 1991), p. 27.

64. The export of U.S. soaps to Europe and of British serials to the United States is well known, but Alessandra Stanley describes a less familiar example of cross-cultural soap watching in "Russians Find Their Heroes in Mexican TV Soap Operas," *New York Times* (March 20, 1994): A1, 8.

65. See Raymond Williams, *Television*, pp. 32–43. See also John Hartley's comment that "the semiotic allegiances of the viewer . . . are both local and global," *Tele-ology: Studies in Television* (London: Routledge, 1992), p. 13; his discussion of viewer demand for locally produced soaps in the essay "Local Television," in the same volume, p. 195; and Edward Buscombe, "Nationhood, Culture and Media Boundaries: Britain," *Quarterly Review of Film and Video* 14, no. 3 (1993): 25–34, especially his remarks on "supra-national" versus locally and regionally produced and oriented programming (pp. 25–26).

66. For another point of difference between British and U.S. serials, see Christine Gledhill's discussion in "Speculations on the Relationship between Soap Opera and Melodrama" of the BBC's specific choice of the realistic over the melodramatic mode when developing its first serials, p. 117. See also Allen, "Bursting Bubbles."

67. For discussions of these series, see Sasha Torres, "Melodrama, Masculinity and the Family: *thirtysomething* as Therapy," *Camera Obscura*, no. 19 (January 1989): 86–106; Elspeth Probyn, "New Traditionalism and Post-Feminism: TV Does the Home," *Screen* 31, no. 2 (Summer 1990): 147–59; and Judith Mayne, "*L.A. Law* and Prime-Time Feminism," *Discourse* 10, no. 2 (Spring-Summer 1988): 48–61. On viewers' intense investment in them, see "Why We Are Still Watching 'thirtysomething,'" *Entertainment Weekly*, no. 12 (May 4, 1990): 78–87; and Lewis Cole, "The Stuff of Real Life," *The Nation* (April 29, 1991): 567–72.

68. Geraghty, "The Continuous Serial," pp. 13–16.

69. Ellis, *Visible Fictions*, pp. 154–59.

70. Raymond Williams cautions in *Television* against confusing "the cultural importance of the serial, as an essentially new form," with the high-culture "ratification" it receives when, in contrast to its frequent use in soap opera, it appears in such series as *Masterpiece Theatre* (p. 61).

71. Gledhill, "Speculations on the Relationship between Soap Opera and Melodrama," pp. 112, 122.

72. For some critics, this cycle of interruption is part of what marks soap opera as a peculiarly "feminine" form of discourse. See for example Brown, "The Politics of Soaps," and Mary Ellen Brown and Linda Barwick, "Fables and Endless Genealogies: Soap Opera and Women's Culture," *Continuum* 1, no. 2 (1988): 71–82. In contrast, Deborah D. Rogers argues, in "Daze of Our Lives: The Soap Opera as Feminine Text," *Journal of American Culture* 14, no. 4 (Winter 1991), that "the fragmented form of soap operas enhances audience receptivity to conservative messages that reinforce stereotypical behavior in women" (p. 29). Other considerations of "feminine discourse" on television include Jackie Byars, "Reading Feminine Discourse: Prime-Time Television in the U.S.," *Communication* 9, no. 3–4 (1987): 289–303; and Fiske, *Television Culture*, pp. 179–97.

73. Judith Mayne analyzes this resonance in "*L.A. Law* and Prime-Time Lesbianism," paper presented at the first annual conference, Console-ing Passions: Television, Video, and Feminism, April 1992, Iowa City, Iowa.

74. Brunsdon, "*Crossroads*," p. 78.

75. Allen, *Speaking of Soap Operas*, p. 15.

76. Porter, "Soap Time," p. 786.

77. Gledhill, "Speculations on the Relationship between Soap Opera and Melodrama," p. 114; Allen, *Speaking of Soap Operas*, p. 74.

78. It may also be one of the most successful, as Allen contends in *Speaking of Soap Operas*: "In the soap opera advertisers and broadcasters have found the ideal vehicle for the reinforcement of advertising impressions and the best means yet devised for assuring regular viewing" (p. 47).

79. For comments by various industry executives on the notion of "appointment television" and the declining importance of being number one in the overall ratings, see Thomas Tryer, "The Fall Season: Network Preview,"

Electronic Media 10, no. 35 (August 26, 1991): 16, and Thomas Tryer and William Mahoney, "Sagansky: CBS Poised for a No. 1 Season," p. 30; and Bill Carter, "NBC Thinks Being No. 1 Is Too Costly," *New York Times* (January 20, 1992): C1–2.

80. Brunsdon, *"Crossroads,"* p. 81.

81. Cf. Meaghan Morris's contribution to the "Spectatrix" issue of *Camera Obscura*, no. 20–21: 241–45. See also Mimi White's discussion of soap operas in her *Tele-Advising: Therapeutic Discourse in American Television* (Chapel Hill: University of North Carolina Press, 1992), pp. 15–18.

82. Annette Kuhn, "Women's Genres: Melodrama, Soap Opera and Theory," in Gledhill, *Home Is Where the Heart Is*, p. 343.

83. During the 1991–92 season, for example, ABC's *Roseanne* was frequently the number one show among both male and female viewers aged 18 to 49 (and the number two show overall, behind *60 Minutes*). While only special broadcasts like the Academy Awards pushed the sitcom out of first place among those women, sporting events televised on one of the major commercial networks regularly ranked number one among men in the same demographic group. During the week of April 6 through April 12, 1992, for instance, *Roseanne* had a Nielsen ranking of number one among women aged 18 to 49, while CBS's broadcast of the NCAA Basketball Championships and the related special, *Prelude to a Championship*, ranked number one and number two among men aged 18 to 49. See "Prime-time Demographics for April 6–12," *Electronic Media* 11, no. 16 (April 20, 1991): 40.

84. Cf. Christine Geraghty's claim that "in their themes and presentation," the programs she identifies as soap operas "seem to offer a space for women in peak viewing time," *Women and Soap Opera*, p. 2.

3. Public Exposure

1. Dennis Porter, "Soap Time: Thoughts on a Commodity Art Form," *College English* 38, no. 8 (April 1977): 786.

2. Charlotte Brunsdon, "*Crossroads*: Notes on Soap Opera," in *Regarding Television: Critical Approaches—An Anthology*, ed. E. Ann Kaplan (Los Angeles: American Film Institute/University Publications of America, 1983), p. 78. See also Mary Ellen Brown and Linda Barwick, "Fables and Endless Genealogies: Soap Opera and Women's Culture," *Continuum* 1, no. 2 (1988): 71–82; and Tania Modleski, *Loving with a Vengeance: Mass-Produced Fantasies for Women* (New York: Methuen, 1984), pp. 85–109.

3. Among the many studies that examine this current in women's history, two of the germinal texts are Ray Strachey, *The Cause: A Short History of the Women's Movement in Great Britain* (1928; rpt. London: Virago, 1978), and Eleanor Flexner, *Century of Struggle: The Woman's Rights Movement in the United States* (1959; rpt. New York: Atheneum, 1968).

4. Nancy Fraser, "What's Critical about Critical Theory? The Case of Habermas and Gender," in *Unruly Practices: Power, Discourse and Gender in Contemporary Social Theory* (Minneapolis: University of Minnesota Press, 1989), p. 122.

5. Nancy Fraser, "Struggle over Needs: Outline of a Socialist-Feminist Critical Theory of Late Capitalist Political Culture," in *Unruly Practices*, p. 168.

6. Bruce Robbins, "Introduction," *The Phantom Public Sphere*, ed. Bruce Robbins (Minneapolis: University of Minnesota Press, 1993), p. xv.

7. Robbins, "Introduction," p. xxi. Cf. Lauren Berlant's contention that "feminist populism will emerge from the engagement of the female culture industry with the patriarchal public sphere, the place where significant or momentous exchanges of power *are perceived* to take place," "The Female Complaint," *Social Text* 19–20 (Fall 1988): 240.

8. For a fascinating consideration of the flexibility of these spheres, with particular attention to their manipulation in the realm of sexuality, see Phillip Brian Harper, "Playing in the Dark: Privacy, Public Sex, and the Erotics of the Cinema Venue," *Camera Obscura*, no. 30 (May 1992): 93–111.

9. Mimi White, *Tele-advising: Therapeutic Discourse in American Television* (Chapel Hill: University of North Carolina Press, 1992), p. 8.

10. Patrice Petro, "Criminality or Hysteria? Television and the Law," *Discourse* 10, no. 2 (Spring–Summer 1988): 52.

11. Patricia Mellencamp identifies daytime soap operas as "the form which most directly operates [what Deleuze and Guattari call] the virile paranoia of secrecy," *High Anxiety: Catastrophe, Scandal, Age, and Comedy* (Bloomington: Indiana University Press, 1990), p. 242.

12. Porter, "Soap Time," p. 786.

13. John Ellis, *Visible Fictions: Cinema, Television, Video*, rev. ed. (London: Routledge, 1992), p. 113; Lynne Joyrich, "Going through the E/Motions: Gender, Postmodernism, and Affect in Television Studies," *Discourse* 14, no. 1 (Winter 1991–92): 28.

14. In her study of the early discourse around television, Spigel has argued that network programmers, magazine editors, and women consumers alike took advantage of the medium's actual and metaphorical power to bring the public world into the home, a linkage that persists to this day. See *Make Room for TV: Television and the Family Ideal in Postwar America* (Chicago: University of Chicago Press, 1992), esp. pp. 99–135. Among many other references to this connection is Andrea Press's comment that "[t]elevision helps us to bridge the gap between the public and private realms of our lives," *Women Watching Television: Gender, Class, and Generation in the American Television Experience* (Philadelphia: University of Pennsylvania Press, 1991), p. 17.

15. See Jeremy G. Butler, "Notes on the Soap Opera Apparatus: Televisual Style and 'As the World Turns,'" *Cinema Journal* 25, no. 3 (Spring 1986): 57.

16. All quotations are my own transcriptions from program broadcasts.

17. Lynne Joyrich, "All That Television Allows: TV Melodrama, Postmodernism and Consumer Culture," *Camera Obscura*, no. 16 (January 1988): 131.

18. Christine Geraghty, *Women and Soap Opera: A Study of Prime Time Soaps* (Cambridge, UK: Polity Press, 1991), p. 53.

19. Geraghty, *Women and Soap Opera*, p. 54.

20. Christine Gledhill, "Speculations on the Relationship between Soap Opera and Melodrama," *Quarterly Review of Film and Video* 14, no. 1–2 (1992): 108.

21. Ellen Seiter, "Promise and Contradiction: The Daytime Television Serial," *Film Studies* 5 (1982): 155.

22. Mimi White, *Tele-advising*, p. 75; subsequent references cited in text. See also Paolo Carpignano, Robin Andersen, Stanley Aronowitz, and William DiPazio, "Chatter in the Age of Electronic Reproduction: Talk Television and the 'Public Mind,'" in Robbins, *The Phantom Public Sphere*, especially their remark that "[t]he mandatory parade of celebrities [on daytime talk shows] does not exclude the emphasis on the personal. In fact, the very rule of television exposure mandates the revelation of the intimate, ordinary side of stardom" (p. 109).

23. While she does not draw the parallel, Sasha Torres notes a similar instance on the ABC drama *thirtysomething* that she describes as highlighting "the issue of individual privacy vs. collective gossip," "Melodrama, Masculinity and the Family: *thirtysomething* as Therapy," *Camera Obscura*, no. 19 (January 1989): 94.

24. Although both depend on viewers' sense of hearing what is usually kept hidden, the pleasures White describes are quite different from the ones offered by the anchors' conversations analyzed by Deborah Schaffer in "Conversing Privately in Public: Patterns of Interaction in *Today* Show Co-op Conversations," *Journal of Popular Culture* 25, no. 3 (Winter 1991): 151–62.

25. Robert C. Allen, *Speaking of Soap Operas* (Chapel Hill: University of North Carolina Press, 1985), p. 74. William Galperin contends that soap operas move forward through "crises of disclosure" rather than "crises of behavior," "Sliding Off the Stereotype: Gender Difference in the Future of Television," in *Postmodernism and Its Discontents: Theories, Practices*, ed. E. Ann Kaplan (London: Verso, 1988), p. 158. See also Christine Gledhill's discussion of soap talk in "Speculations on the Relationship between Soap Opera and Melodrama," pp. 111, 114–15; and Christine Geraghty's analysis of gossip in "The Continuous Serial—A Definition," in *Coronation Street*, ed. Richard Dyer, Christine Geraghty, Marion Jordan, Terry Lovell, Richard Paterson, and John Stewart (London: British Film Institute, 1981), pp. 22–24.

26. Joy V. Fuqua explores the evolution of this story in "'There's a Queer in My Soap!': The AIDS/Homophobia Storyline of *One Life to Live*," in *To Be Continued . . . Soap Operas around the World*, ed. Robert C. Allen (London: Routledge, forthcoming).

27. Peter Brooks, *The Melodramatic Imagination: Balzac, Henry James, Melodrama, and the Mode of Excess* (New Haven: Yale University Press, 1976), p. 4.

28. See Brooks, *The Melodramatic Imagination*, p. 35; Robert Lang, *American Film Melodrama: Griffith, Vidor, Minelli* (Princeton: Princeton University Press, 1989), p. 50; and Christine Gledhill, "Speculations on the Relationship between Soap Opera and Melodrama," pp. 108–109.

29. Joyrich, "All That Television Allows," p. 139.

30. Dorothy Hobson has gone even farther, arguing that viewers are actually "in a superior position to the producers," "Soap Operas at Work," in *Remote Control: Television, Audiences, and Cultural Power*, ed. Ellen Seiter, Hans Borchers, Gabriele Kreutzner, and Eva-Maria Warth (London: Routledge, 1989), p. 167.

31. Contrary to Deborah D. Rogers's contention in "Daze of Our Lives: The Soap Opera as Feminine Text," *Journal of American Culture* 14, no. 4 (Winter 1991), that viewers are "[i]nformed of everyone's secrets" and are "guaranteed accurate knowledge" (p. 30), some information may be kept from viewers until the last moment.

32. Modleski, *Loving with a Vengeance*, p. 91; Rogers, "Daze of Our Lives," p. 30; David Buckingham, *Public Secrets: EastEnders and Its Audience* (London: BFI Publishing, 1987), pp. 63–64, 82.

33. John Hartley, "Out of Bounds: The Myth of Marginality," in *Television Mythologies: Stars, Shows and Signs*, ed. Len Masterman (London: Comedia, 1984), p. 124. See also his introduction to *Tele-ology: Studies in Television* (London: Routledge, 1992), in which he contrasts "*paedocratic* audience practices" with "pedagogic interventions" (p. 17).

34. Gloria-Jean Masciarotte, "C'mon Girl: Oprah Winfrey and the Discourse of Feminine Talk," *Genders* 11 (Fall 1991): 85; subsequent references cited in text.

35. Spigel, *Make Room for TV*, p. 129.

36. Spigel, *Make Room for TV*, p. 132.

37. Buckingham, *Public Secrets*, p. 164.

38. Buckingham, *Public Secrets*, p. 200. For a more detailed discussion of the function of viewers' gossip about soap operas, at least among British fans, see Dorothy Hobson, "Soap Operas at Work."

39. Feuer, "Narrative Form in American Network Television," p. 112.

40. Patricia Meyer Spacks, *Gossip* (Chicago: University of Chicago Press, 1986), p. 67; subsequent references cited in text.

41. Joyrich, "All That Television Allows," p. 147.

42. Geraghty, *Women and Soap Opera*, p. 102.

43. Buckingham, *Public Secrets*, p. 90.

44. Thomas Elsaesser, "Tales of Sound and Fury: Observations on the Family Melodrama," in *Home Is Where the Heart Is: Studies in Melodrama and the Woman's Film*, ed. Christine Gledhill (London: British Film Institute, 1987), p. 47.

4. How Things End

1. Robert C. Allen, "On Reading Soaps: A Semiotic Primer," in *Regarding Television: Critical Approaches—An Anthology*, ed. E. Ann Kaplan (Los Angeles: American Film Institute/University Publications of America, 1983), p. 98. See also his claim that the soap opera "is predicated upon the infinite delay of closure," "Bursting Bubbles: 'Soap Opera,' Audiences, and the Limits of Genre," in *Remote Control: Television, Audiences, and Cultural Power*, ed. Ellen Seiter, Hans Borchers, Gabriele Kreutzner, and Eva-Maria Warth (London: Routledge, 1989), p. 48; and similar statements throughout *Speaking of Soap Operas* (Chapel Hill: University of North Carolina Press, 1985).

2. Dennis Porter, "Soap Time: Thoughts on a Commodity Art Form," *College English* 38, no. 8 (April 1977): 783. In "Melodrama, Serial Form

and Television Today," *Screen* 25, no. 1 (January–February 1984), Jane Feuer makes a similar observation of prime-time serials: "the only moral imperative of the continuing serial form [is that] the plot must go on" (p. 12).

3. Jerry Palmer, *Potboilers: Methods, Concepts and Case Studies in Popular Fiction* (London: Routledge, 1991), p. 7.

4. Susan Willis, *A Primer for Everday Life* (New York: Routledge, 1991), p. 5. Among the many other analyses whose argument rests on the assumption that soap opera storylines do not achieve closure, see Martha Nochimson, *No End to Her: Soap Opera and the Female Subject* (Berkeley: University of California Press, 1992), pp. 42, 79, 118, 144–45, and passim.

5. Christine Geraghty, "The Continuous Serial—A Definition," in *Coronation Street*, ed. Richard Dyer, Christine Geraghty, Marion Jordan, Terry Lovell, Richard Paterson, and John Stewart (London: British Film Institute, 1981), pp. 11, 15.

6. Sandy Flitterman-Lewis, "All's Well That Doesn't End: Soap Operas and the Marriage Motif," *Camera Obscura*, no. 16 (January 1988): 127, 120.

7. Jeremy Butler, "Notes on the Soap Opera Apparatus: Televisual Style and 'As the World Turns,'" *Cinema Journal* 25, no. 3 (Spring 1986): 54.

8. Lynne Joyrich, "All That Television Allows: TV Melodrama, Postmodernism and Consumer Culture," *Camera Obscura*, no. 16 (January 1988): 140.

9. Palmer, *Potboilers*, p. 7.

10. Henry Jenkins, *Textual Poachers: Television Fans and Participatory Culture* (New York: Routledge, 1992), especially pp. 162–77.

11. Christine Geraghty, *Women and Soap Opera: A Study of Prime Time Soaps* (Cambridge: Polity Press, 1991), p. 170.

12. Verina Glaessner, "Gendered Fictions," in *Understanding Television*, ed. Andrew Goodwin and Garry Whannel (London: Routledge, 1991), p. 118.

13. See Brad Chisholm's description of "the difficult text" in "Difficult Viewing: The Pleasures of Complex Screen Narratives," *Critical Studies in Mass Communication* 8, no. 4 (December 1991): 389–403.

14. Sandy Flitterman[-Lewis], "The *Real* Soap Operas: TV Commercials," in Kaplan, *Regarding Television*, p. 94.

15. D. A. Miller, *Narrative and Its Discontents: Problems of Closure in the Traditional Novel* (Princeton: Princeton University Press, 1981), p. ix.

16. Steven Cohan and Linda M. Shires, *Telling Stories: A Theoretical Analysis of Narrative Fiction* (New York: Routledge, 1988), p. 82. Cf. Ien Ang's description of soap operas as having an "excessive plot structure," "Melodramatic Identifications: Television Fiction and Women's Fantasy," in *Television and Women's Culture*, ed. Mary Ellen Brown (London: Sage, 1990), p. 79; and Robert Allen's description of "over-coding" in "On Reading Soaps," pp. 103–104.

17. Allen, *Speaking of Soap Operas*, p. 92.

18. See Jane Feuer, "The Concept of Live Television: Ontology as Ideology," in Kaplan, *Regarding Television*, pp. 12–22.

19. See Deborah D. Rogers, "Daze of Our Lives: The Soap Opera as Feminine Text," *Journal of American Culture* 14, no. 4 (Winter 1991): 30.

20. Tony Bennett and Janet Woollacott, *Bond and Beyond: The Political Career of a Popular Hero* (London: Macmillan Education, 1987), p. 70.

21. It is worth noting that by following Bennett and Woollacott's story/ plot distinction, I reverse the one made by David Bordwell, which rests on a theory of narrative altogether different from my own. For the initial distinction, see David Bordwell, Janet Staiger, and Kristin Thompson, *The Classical Hollywood Cinema: Film Style and Mode of Production to 1960* (New York: Columbia University Press, 1985), pp. 12, 24. For Bordwell's revocation of this distinction, see his *Narration in the Fictional Film* (Madison: University of Wisconsin Press, 1985), p. 344n. For a critique of Bordwell's system, see Bill Nichols, "Form Wars: The Political Unconscious of Formalist Theory," *SAQ* 88, no. 2 (Spring 1989): 486–515.

22. In "'Day after Tomorrow': Audience Interaction and Soap Opera Production," *Cultural Critique*, no. 23 (Winter 1992–93), Jennifer Hayward puts this another way:

> Soaps ask: What if we were to have the same plots, only a few of them, at our disposal forever? What if the number and types of characters were limited? What if, admitting this, we made no attempt to hide the fact? Could we make narrative strange, could we make it new, could we bear to keep watching forever? Soaps say yes. (P. 106)

23. As Cohan and Shires explain, "The enigma thus guarantees the story's movement," *Telling Stories*, p. 64. Cf. Roland Barthes's discussion of the hermeneutic code in *S/Z: An Essay*, trans. Richard Miller (New York: Noonday Press/Farrar, Straus & Giroux, 1974), e.g., pp. 17, 19, 209–10, 262.

24. Barthes, *S/Z*, p. 52.

25. Alex McNeil, *Total Television: A Comprehensive Guide to Programming from 1948 to the Present*, 3rd ed. (New York: Penguin Books, 1991), p. 839.

26. To invoke once again the example of *Twin Peaks*, it may be that part of viewers' (and creators'?) genre confusion stemmed from uncertainty about whether the Laura Palmer murder narrative was in fact the series' basic problematic or simply the subject of a story arc.

27. Restated as questions that had to be resolved before closure could be achieved, this arc consists of storylines involving the following enigmas: Will Cassie and Andrew stay together? Will Andrew lose his church position because of his stand on privacy and sexuality? Will Sloan finally be reconciled to his son William's homosexuality and accept William's death from AIDS? Will Marty repent over having spread rumors about Andrew? Will Billy Douglas finally come out to his parents? Will Joey and Alana become a couple? Will Clint and Viki break up? Will Viki have an affair with Sloan? Will Sloan seek proper medical treatment and recover from his apparently terminal illness?

28. Joy V. Fuqua's work makes it clear that the sense of what constitutes the core of a story arc shifts, even within the program's production staff. See "'There's a Queer in My Soap!': The AIDS/Homophobia Storyline of *One Life to Live*," in *To Be Continued . . . Soap Operas around the World*, ed. Robert C. Allen (London: Routledge, forthcoming).

29. One arc may also cross another dramatically without directly affecting the second one's progress. On *The Young and the Restless*, for instance, two simultaneous arcs included romance-oriented storylines focusing on separate tetrads, one involving Victor Newman, his ex-wife Nikki, her husband

Jack Abbott, and Jack's sister Ashley (also Victor's ex-wife) and their over-lapping family and business lives in Jabot Cosmetics and Newman Enter-prises, the other involving the similarly complicated relationships among Olivia Hastings and her husband Nathan, her sister Drucilla Barber, and Drucilla's boyfriend (later husband) Neil Winters. An October 1992 scene demon-strates that an event that properly belongs to one arc can occur within a scene that is actually part of an entirely different arc: Nathan called Neil out of a Newman Enterprises meeting to summon him to the hospital to see the critically ill Olivia. Although these two arcs briefly intersected during the phone call, Neil's departure had no discernable effect on the meeting be-cause the meeting and his visit to Olivia were parts, not merely of different storylines, but of different arcs as well. Had the two storylines—about Olivia's hospitalization and Victor Newman's business dealings—been part of the same arc, we would have expected Neil's sudden departure to have had at least some small impact on the meeting.

30. Ellen Seiter, "Promise and Contradiction: The Daytime Television Serial," *Film Reader* 5 (1982): 158.

31. Barthes, *S/Z*, p. 75.

32. In *High Anxiety: Catastrophe, Scandal, Age, and Comedy* (Bloomington: Indiana University Press, 1992), Patricia Mellencamp sug-gests an entirely different understanding of soap opera resolution as a closure "of *identification* . . . , of masquerade rather than story, of affect rather than effect" (pp. 283–84), providing an opportunity for "satiation/closure" through a particularly intimate view of (women) characters' faces (p. 284) via a typical bit of soap opera camera work: a close-up that replaces the con-ventional shot–reverse shot with a simultaneous shot of two women facing the camera during a conversation, so that we see both women at once.

33. Dorothy Hobson, *"Crossroads": The Drama of a Soap Opera* (Lon-don: Methuen, 1982), p. 35. Caren J. Deming makes a similar claim in "For Television-Centred Television Criticism: Lessons from Feminism," in Brown, *Television and Women's Culture*, when she writes that "the moment of narra-tive closure in soap operas is more like a pause for breath. Closure in a soap always threatens to come unstuck, as indeed it sometimes does" (p. 56).

34. Jane Feuer, "Narrative Form in American Network Television," in *High Theory/Low Culture: Analysing Popular Television and Film*, ed. Colin MacCabe (New York: St. Martin's Press, 1986), p. 112.

35. There are similarities between the strategies Barthes calls "partial" or "suspended answers" (*S/Z*, pp. 75, 210) and what I identify here as tempo-rary closure, but I choose to employ the latter term because of its currency among soap opera theorists and critics.

36. In "Melodrama, Serial Form and Television Today," Jane Feuer links temporary closure on *Dallas* and *Dynasty* to those programs' "moments of melodramatic excess," which "occur as a form of temporary closure within and between episodes and even entire seasons" (p. 12).

37. Lauren Rabinovitz has discussed the practice of suspending ongoing storylines in connection with soaps' increasingly lavish weddings and the fan magazine discourse that accompanies them in "Soap Opera Bridal Fanta-sies," *Screen* 33, no. 3 (Autumn 1992): 274–83. But while Rabinovitz pre-sents these heavily promoted spectacles as essentially tools to attract viewers

during the ratings sweeps periods (February, May, August, and November) that determine advertising revenues, such interruptions are by no means confined to those months, as even her own examples make clear.

38. As chapter 3 should have made clear, however, this practice is distinct from the closely related one of setting an entire episode's events in a particular, usually public setting, such as a large social gathering. For example, the June 24, 1994, episode of *General Hospital* took place at a fund-raising ball, but rather than focusing the whole hour on a single story, the ongoing events in several different storylines were simply played out in public.

39. John Ellis, *Visible Fictions: Cinema, Television, Video*, rev. ed. (London: Routledge, 1992), p. 156. Cf. John Caughie's description of television in general as "a narrative structure that need not end (because not driven by causality), but which, if it does end, may end arbitrarily," "Adorno's Reproach: Repetition, Difference and Television Genre," *Screen* 32, no. 2 (Summer 1991): 145. An obvious exception to these arguments, which neither Ellis nor Caughie raises, is the finale of certain episodic series— such as the one that famously concluded *The Fugitive*—that do directly attempt to resolve the series' basic problematic. For a discussion of closure techniques in recent series finales and their implications for television aesthetics, see M. S. Piccirillo, "On the Authenticity of Televisual Experience: A Critical Exploration of Para-Social Closure," *Critical Studies in Mass Communication* 3, no. 3 (September 1986): 337–55. As Piccirillo points out, television conventions with regard to series endings change, and the current trend is for programs to provide "conclusions" rather than simply ceasing production (p. 347).

40. Ellis, *Visible Fictions*, p. 154. Even his claim that "[t]he characteristic form of series narration is that of the continuous update" (p. 158) is as descriptive of soaps as of conventional series television. It is important to note, however, that because he is writing about British television forms, Ellis's terms do not apply smoothly to U.S. examples. He specifically counts soap operas among his examples of series, reserving the term "serial" for limited-run episodic programs, what U.S. viewers would probably think of as miniseries (p. 123). He appears, however, to be referring to British serials like *Coronation Street*, rather than to U.S. daytime soaps (pp. 148–49).

41. It is worth noting that the networks themselves seem increasingly to highlight individual storylines in their promotion of specific soap operas, even going so far as to isolate and name particular stories in on-air and print ad campaigns. ABC, for instance, promoted a crossover storyline in which characters moved from one program to another, with ads that read "'Fatal Connection': *All My Children* comes to *Loving*" (*Soap Opera Weekly* 3, no. 42 [October 20, 1992]: 11; *Soap Opera Magazine* 2, no. 43 [October 20, 1992]: 47; and *Soap Opera Digest* 17, no. 22 [October 27, 1992]: 127). Another campaign, which ran in both fan magazines and on-air network spots, singled out a storyline involving Erica Kane's visit to Budapest and her subsequent kidnapping by her lover's half-brother as "'Destiny on the Danube,' a special on-location presentation beginning October 29" (*Soap Opera Weekly* 3, no. 43 [October 27, 1992]: 110). Earlier in the fall, CBS ran similar campaigns for crossover stories on *The Bold and the Beautiful* and *The Young and the Restless*.

42. Barthes, *S/Z*, pp. 187–88, 209.

43. Peter Brooks, *Reading for the Plot: Design and Intention in Narrative* (New York: Alfred A. Knopf, 1984), p. 104.

44. Stephen Neale, *Genre* (London: British Film Institute, 1980), p. 30.

45. Neale, *Genre*, p. 26.

46. Tania Modleski, *Loving with a Vengeance: Mass-Produced Fantasies for Women* (New York: Methuen, 1984), p. 88.

47. Cohan and Shires, *Telling Stories*, p. 1.

48. Edward Branigan, *Narrative Comprehension and Film* (London: Routledge, 1992), p. 4.

49. Claims about the ideological function of traditional methods of closure have not, of course, been limited to film. Indeed, film theorists like Colin MacCabe initially drew on novels to articulate the notion of the "classic realist text," and literary critics have continued to engage the issue. For instance, Rachel Blau DuPlessis's influential *Writing beyond the Ending: Narrative Strategies of Twentieth-Century Women Writers* (Bloomington: Indiana University Press, 1985) focuses on women writers' attempts to move beyond traditional and ideologically loaded narrative resolutions in order to reimagine women's lives. "Narrative outcome," she writes, "is one place where transindividual assumptions and values are most clearly visible" (p. 3). For a more recent feminist consideration of literary closure, see Alison Booth, ed., *Famous Last Words: Changes in Gender and Narrative Closure* (Charlottesville: University of Virginia Press, 1993).

50. Feuer, "Melodrama, Serial Form and Television Today," p. 8; subsequent references cited in text.

51. Feuer, "Narrative Form in American Network Television," p. 102.

52. Deming, "For Television-Centred Television Criticism," p. 49.

53. Caughie, "Adorno's Reproach," pp. 141, 145.

54. John Fiske, "Popular Narrative and Commercial Television," *Camera Obscura*, no. 23 (May 1990): 133–47.

55. Deming, "For Television-Centred Television Criticism," p. 45.

56. John Fiske, *Television Culture* (London: Methuen, 1987), pp. 179–84 and passim. See also Nochimson, *No End to Her*, pp. 2, 4, and passim; and Palmer, *Potboilers*, pp. 162–63. In "C'mon Girl: Oprah Winfrey and the Discourse of Feminine Talk," *Genders* 11 (Fall 1991), Gloria-Jean Masciarotte suggests that daytime talk shows offer a similar form of enjoyment for their largely female audiences, arguing that "[t]he talk show's own continuance depends on its denial of the narrative closure and narrative authority" (p. 92).

57. Barbara Klinger, "'Cinema/Ideology/Criticism' Revisited: The Progressive Text," *Screen* 25, no. 1 (January–February 1984): 41.

58. Andrew Goodwin makes a similar argument about pop music in *Dancing in the Distraction Factory: Music Television and Popular Culture* (Minneapolis: University of Minnesota Press, 1992), pp. 74–78.

59. See Deborah Rogers, "Daze of Our Lives," pp. 29, 32. Cf. Jane Feuer's conclusion in "Melodrama, Serial Form and Television Today," that prime-time serials bear "what appears to be a right-wing ideology by means of a potentially progressive narrative form" (p. 16).

60. Geraghty, *Women and Soap Opera*, p. 122.

61. Charlotte Brunsdon, "Writing about Soap Opera," in *Television Mythologies: Stars, Shows and Signs*, ed. Len Masterman (London: Comedia, 1984), p. 83. Despite Brunsdon's acknowledgment of the pleasures of anticipation, however, in the same essay she locates the appeal of British programs like *Coronation Street* elsewhere: "it is surely the predictable familiarity of the life represented which pulls us in," especially the fact that the form's "generic lack of closure in combination with the realist premise, offers a homology between soap-life and viewer life" (p. 86).

62. In *Bond and Beyond*, Bennett and Woollacott make a related point about Bond fans who, they claim, experience a pleasurable tension between suspense and the comforting foreknowledge "that, in the end, all will be well" (p. 94). Similarly, in *Adventure, Mystery, and Romance: Formula Stories as Art and Popular Culture* (Chicago: University of Chicago Press, 1976), John G. Cawelti points to this tension as "[o]ne of the major sources of Hitchcock's effects," which include "the tension between our hope that things will be properly resolved and our suspicion that Hitchcock might suddenly dump us out of the moral fantasy in which mysteries are always solved" (pp. 17–18). See also Janice Radway's discovery that the women she describes often read a book's ending first, in *Reading the Romance: Women, Patriarchy, and Popular Literature* (Chapel Hill: University of North Carolina Press, 1984), p. 99.

63. Palmer, *Potboilers*, p. 162.

64. Frederic Jameson, "Reification and Utopia in Mass Culture," in *Signatures of the Visible* (New York: Routledge, 1990), p. 13.

65. Brooks, *Reading for the Plot*, p. 22.

66. Bill Nichols makes this claim of David Bordwell in "Form Wars," pp. 494, 498, 507.

67. Dorothy Hobson has been one of the few critics to suggest a specifically ideological—indeed, patriarchal—function for the resolution of soap opera plots, claiming that "[i]t is in the forms that the resolutions are made within programmes [like the British serials *Coronation Street* and *Crossroads*] that the ideological basis of consensual femininity is *reproduced* and *reinforced* for women," "Housewives and the Mass Media," in *Culture, Media, Language: Working Papers in Cultural Studies, 1972–1979*, ed. Stuart Hall, Dorothy Hobson, Andrew Lowe, and Paul Willis (London: Hutchinson, 1980), p. 113.

68. As Joy Fuqua demonstrates in "'There's a Queer in My Soap!'", stories such as Billy Douglas's coming-out on *One Life to Live* may be resolved in a way that threatens patriarchal certainties—asserting, in this case, a liberal tolerance for homosexuality—but they are then immediately recuperated through the subsequent marginalization of the disruptive characters.

5. Plotting Paternity

1. The most famous exposition of the role of paternity in women's oppression is of course Engels's in *The Origin of the Family, Private Property, and the State*. Among feminist theorists, see for example Simone de Beauvoir,

The Second Sex, trans. H. M. Parshley (New York: Bantam Books, 1961), pp. 61–73; Gerda Lerner, *The Creation of Patriarchy* (Oxford: Oxford University Press, 1986), pp. 149, 185–86; and Peggy Reeves Sanday, *Female Power and Male Dominance: On the Origins of Sexual Inequality* (Cambridge: Cambridge University Press, 1981), esp. chapter 3.

2. Two germinal feminist analyses of the meaning of the exchange of women, both of which address its significance as an enforcer of paternal identity, are Gayle Rubin, "The Traffic in Women: Notes on the 'Political Economy' of Sex," in *Toward an Anthropology of Women*, ed. Rayna R. Reiter (New York: Monthly Review Press, 1975), pp. 157–210; and Juliet Mitchell, *Psychoanalysis and Feminism: Freud, Reich, Laing and Women* (New York: Vintage Books, 1975), pp. 370–81.

3. For example, the homuncule theory claimed that sperm contained complete beings that were simply implanted in women. For some of the implications of the association between women and nature, see Sherry Ortner, "Is Female to Male as Nature Is to Culture?" in *Women, Culture and Society*, ed. Michelle Z. Rosaldo and Louise Lamphere (Stanford: Stanford University Press, 1974), pp. 67–88.

4. Two very different feminist approaches to the mythic quality of male uncertainty over paternity are Jane Gallop, *The Daughter's Seduction: Feminism and Psychoanalysis* (Ithaca: Cornell University Press, 1982), pp. 39, 47; and Mary O'Brien, *The Politics of Reproduction* (Boston: Routledge and Kegan Paul, 1981), pp. 30, 48–49, and passim.

5. Mary Ann Doane, *The Desire to Desire: The Woman's Film of the 1940s* (Bloomington: Indiana University Press, 1987), pp. 70–71.

6. Thomas Elsaesser, "Tales of Sound and Fury: Observations on the Family Melodrama," in *Home Is Where the Heart Is: Studies in Melodrama and the Woman's Film*, ed. Christine Gledhill (London: British Film Institute, 1987), p. 44. Cf. Ien Ang's application of this insight to soap operas, in *Watching "Dallas": Soap Opera and the Melodramatic Imagination*, trans. Delia Couling (London: Methuen, 1985), p. 64.

7. Other critics have, of course, noted the predominance of storylines about paternity, although none has made a sustained argument about the subject's importance to the genre. See, among many others, Ellen Seiter, "Promise and Contradiction: The Daytime Television Serial," *Film Reader* 5 (1982): 154; Christine Geraghty, *Women and Soap Opera: A Study of Prime Time Soaps* (Cambridge, UK: Polity Press, 1991), pp. 68–69; and Patricia Mellencamp, *High Anxiety: Catastrophe, Scandal, Age, and Comedy* (Bloomington: Indiana University Press, 1992), pp. 242–43.

8. "Projected Storyline for The Guiding Light," November 24, 1952, July 31 and October 15, 1953, Irna Phillips Papers, Film and Manuscript Archive, State Historical Society of Wisconsin. Phillips's correspondence with the advertising agency controlling the program also provides evidence that patrilineage was an important source of identity even in these early days. A story about Paul Fletcher, whose parents were unmarried and whose father is unknown, focuses on Paul's conviction that he is no one—because he has no father. At one point, Phillips even draws an explicit parallel between this plot and the Kathy Lang Grant paternity plot. See "Projected Storyline for The Guiding Light," April 27, 1957, pp. 10–14.

9. Tania Modleski, *Loving with a Vengeance: Mass-Produced Fantasies for Women* (New York: Methuen, 1982), pp. 88, 108.

10. Janice Radway, *Reading the Romance: Women, Patriarchy, and Popular Literature* (Chapel Hill: University of North Carolina Press, 1984), p. 148.

11. Mimi White argues that this kind of "retrofitting" is an important characteristic of soap opera narrative. See her "Women, Memory, and Serial Melodrama: Rewriting/Reviewing History," paper delivered at the second annual conference, Console-ing Passions: Television, Video, and Feminism, Los Angeles, April 1993, from which my later page references come.

12. See Modleski, *Loving with a Vengeance*, p. 95.

13. Mimi White calls this the "romantic incest plot," in "Women, Memory, and History," p. 36. See also Louise Spence, "Family, Limits, and Desire: Incest on Daytime Soap Operas," paper presented at the third annual conference, Console-ing Passions: Television, Video, and Feminism, Tucson, April 1994.

14. Elsaesser, "Tales of Sound and Fury," p. 64.

15. All quotations are my transcriptions from program broadcasts.

16. See for example Nancy Chodorow, *The Reproduction of Mothering: Psychoanalysis and the Sociology of Gender* (Berkeley: University of California Press, 1978); and the writings of Adrienne Rich and Sarah Ruddick, among others.

17. See for example Radway, *Reading the Romance*, p. 141.

18. Contrast Ien Ang's comment that "[f]amily is not actually romanticized in soap operas; on the contrary, the imaginary ideal of the family as safe haven in a heartless world is constantly shattered," *Watching "Dallas,"* p. 69.

19. Hilary Radner, "Quality Television and Feminine Narcissism: The Shrew and the Covergirl," *Genders* 8 (Summer 1990): 123.

20. Radway, *Reading the Romance*, pp. 214–15.

21. Laura Mulvey, "Notes on Sirk and Melodrama," in Gledhill, *Home Is Where the Heart Is*, p. 75.

22. Mulvey, "Notes on Sirk and Melodrama," p. 75.

23. As Martha Nochimson points out, the project of tracking soap opera history is frustrated by the lack of archival resources. See *No End to Her: Soap Opera and the Female Subject* (Berkeley: University of California Press, 1993), p. 198.

6. Beyond Soap Opera

1. Deborah D. Rogers discusses some of these instances in "Daze of Our Lives: The Soap Opera as Feminine Text," *Journal of American Culture* 14, no. 4 (Winter 1991): 29–41.

2. David Morley, *Television, Audiences and Cultural Studies* (London: Routledge, 1992), p. 26.

3. For a consideration of this problem from the perspective of African American audiences, see the analyses of two controversial media artifacts: Jacqueline Bobo, "*The Color Purple*: Black Women as Cultural Readers," in *Female Spectators: Looking at Film and Television*, ed. E. Deidre Pribram (Lon-

don: Verso, 1988), pp. 90–109; and Sut Jhally and Justin Lewis, *Enlightened Racism: "The Cosby Show," Audiences, and the Myth of the American Dream* (Boulder: Westview Press, 1992).

4. Bobo, "*The Color Purple*," p. 101.

5. Morley, *Television, Audiences and Cultural Studies*, p. 26; see also Patricia Mellencamp, *Indiscretions: Avant-Garde Film, Video, and Feminism* (Bloomington: Indiana University Press, 1990).

6. Robert C. Allen, *Speaking of Soap Operas* (Chapel Hill: University of North Carolina Press, 1985), p. 88.

7. Madeleine Edmondson and David Rounds, *From Mary Noble to Mary Hartman: The Complete Soap Opera Book* (New York: Stein and Day, 1976), call *Daytime Serial Newsletter* "the magazine that originated the concept of chronicling the day-to-day activities of the soaps" (p. 173). For an introduction to fan culture, including the production of publications like the early soap newsletters, see Henry Jenkins, *Textual Poachers: Television Fans and Participatory Culture* (New York: Routledge, 1992).

8. Dorothy Hobson documents the way that women talk about soap operas among themselves in "Soap Operas at Work," in *Remote Control: Television, Audiences, and Cultural Power*, ed. Ellen Seiter, Hans Borchers, Gabriele Kreutzner, and Eva-Maria Warth (London: Routledge, 1989), pp. 150–67; and "Women Audiences and the Workplace," in *Television and Women's Culture: The Politics of the Popular*, ed. Mary Ellen Brown (London: Sage Publications, 1990), pp. 61–71.

9. For an account of British newspaper and magazine coverage of serials like *Coronation Street* and *Crossroads*, see Dorothy Hobson, *"Crossroads": The Drama of a Soap Opera* (London: Methuen, 1982), pp. 13–25. More recently, the growing popularity of British serials and imports from the United States and Australia has spawned a new commercially produced magazine, *Inside Soap* (Attic Futura Ltd.).

10. John Fiske, *Television Culture* (New York: Methuen, 1987), p. 118.

11. Nielsen ratings, week of May 9–13, 1994, *Soap Opera Weekly* 5, no. 23 (June 7, 1994): 9; circulation figures, *Ulrich's International Periodicals Directory, 1993–94*, vol. 1 (New Providence, NJ: Bowker, 1993), pp. 1573, 1556. In comparison, *Ulrich's* reports that the Florida-based Spanish-language fan magazine *TV y novelas* has a circulation of 1.2 million (p. 1575); the British *Doctor Who Magazine*, 25,000 (p. 1565); *Star Trek: The Official Fan Club Magazine*, 105,000 (p. 1574). *TV Guide* has a circulation of 15.8 million (p. 1574).

12. "Critical Condition," *Soap Opera Weekly* 4, no. 5 (February 2, 1993): 18.

13. Mimi Torchin, "Speaking My Mind," *Soap Opera Weekly* 3, no. 46 (November 17, 1992): 4. Cf. the controversy over the genre definition of Norman Lear's satire *Mary Hartman, Mary Hartman* in the early days of soap newsletters and magazines, described in Edmondson and Rounds, *From Mary Noble to Mary Hartman*, pp. 171–76.

14. K. McHugh, *Soap Opera Weekly* 4, no. 4 (January 26, 1993): 42.

15. "Critical Condition," *Soap Opera Weekly* 4, no. 4 (January 26, 1993): 18.

16. *Soap Opera Magazine* 3, no. 2 (January 12, 1993): 10–45. Similar

features include *Soap Opera Weekly*'s two-part "For Your Consideration," listing actresses and actors "who deserve Emmy nominations," 3, no. 50 (December 15, 1992): 11–15 and no. 51 (December 22, 1992): 12–14.

17. "Not many people know it, but the words 'super couple'—universally used in the daytime serial industry—were actually coined in the offices of *Soap Opera Digest* in 1984," "The Origin of Super Couples," *Soap Opera Digest Extra!: Soap Opera Super Couples Special* (Summer 1992): 65.

18. For instance, "Objects of Desire: Daytime's Nine Most Wanted Lovers," *Soap Opera Update* 6, no. 2 (January 12, 1993): 33–41.

19. *Soap Opera Weekly* 3, no. 44 (November 3, 1993): 12–15.

20. *Soap Opera Digest* 18, no. 7 (March 30, 1993): 100–110; subsequent references cited in text.

21. Cf. Fiske, *Television Culture*, pp. 119–20; Allen, *Speaking of Soap Operas*, p. 89.

22. *Soap Opera Weekly* 4, no. 4 (January 26, 1993): 36–38.

23. *Soap Opera Digest* 18, no. 2 (January 19, 1993): 22–26. This story also includes a sidebar called "Good Reps," listing "ten soap stars you'll never hear a bad word about" (p. 26).

24. For an insider's view of how soap opera production practices create this sense of an "unauthored" text, see Martha Nochimson, *No End to Her: Soap Opera and the Female Subject* (Berkeley: University of California Press, 1993), pp. 5–8.

25. On viewer interest in this particular aspect of soap opera production, see Lauren Rabinowitz, "Soap Opera Bridal Fantasies," *Screen* 33, no. 3 (Autumn 1992): 274–83.

26. "Sneak Peaks at a *GH* Rehearsal," *Episodes* (November–December 1992): 18–19; and Jim Warren, "Behind the Scenes at General Hospital," *Soap Opera Weekly* 4, no. 4 (January 26, 1993): 32–33.

27. John Fiske, "The Cultural Economy of Fandom," in *The Adoring Audience: Fan Culture and Popular Media*, ed. Lisa A. Lewis (London: Routledge, 1992), p. 40.

28. See Jenkins, *Textual Poachers*, pp. 81–82.

29. Fiske, *Television Culture*, p. 123.

30. *Soap Opera Weekly* 4, no. 5 (February 2, 1993): 20; subsequent references cited in text.

31. A similar report appeared in that same date's issue of *Soap Opera Magazine* 3, no. 5 (February 2, 1993), couched in terms that still left room for viewers to speculate about the details of the scene: "Barbara Rush leaves her role as NOLA January 28 in a three-hankie final scene with TAD. The actress will continue to appear in flashbacks" (p. 9). This does not, however, represent a significant difference in the approaches of the two magazines, for other *Soap Opera Magazine* announcements have been as detailed as those in *Soap Opera Weekly*.

32. A. Vickers and Mimi Torchin, *Soap Opera Weekly* 4, no. 6 (February 9, 1993): 42. Interestingly, this kind of response to viewer complaints seems to mark the limit of soap magazines' concern about giving away plot turns prematurely. The November 24, 1992, issue of *Soap Opera Digest* (17, no. 24), for instance, carried the caption "Oops! Stories We Shouldn't Have Told." However, the feature itself—"Stories That Are None of Our Busi-

ness," pp. 10–13—turns out to be about real and hypothetical *personal* revelations the magazine's editors think they had no right to make, largely having to do with performers' unannounced pregnancies, substance-abuse problems, conflicts on the sets of individual shows, and so on. There is no mention of story-related revelations.

33. Charlotte Brunsdon, "Writing about Soap Opera," in *Television Mythologies: Stars, Shows & Signs*, ed. Len Masterman (London: Comedia, 1984), p. 83.

34. Soap opera fans continue to create new ways of interacting with and around the text, including fan groups organized on computer networks and bulletin boards. See Lauren Rabinovitz, "All My Computers: The Electronic World of Reception in Soap Opera Nets," paper presented at the third annual conference, Console-ing Passions: Television, Video, and Feminism, April 1994, Tucson.

35. On the inherent difficulties of such integration, Robert C. Allen writes,

> The problem of including blacks and other racial groups in soaps is not one of working them into plot lines, but dealing with the paradigmatic consequences of their entry into the community of the soap opera world. . . . Unless a particular soap were to embrace interracial marriage and parentage as a community norm, the admission of a nonwhite character into full membership in the soap community would be impossible.

See "*The Guiding Light*: Soap Opera as Economic Product and Cultural Document," in *Television: The Critical View*, 4th ed., ed. Horace Newcomb (New York: Oxford University Press, 1987), pp. 156–57.

36. Terry Lovell suggests a similar way of imagining the extent to which a program's ideology could shift without fundamentally altering its appeal: "A good practical exercise for study groups would be to attempt to rewrite an episode or storyline . . . within the constraints of the genre, from a feminist or socialist perspective, without losing the qualities which make *Coronation Street* so pleasurable and popular," "Ideology and *Coronation Street*," in *Coronation Street*, ed. Richard Dyer, Christine Geraghty, Marion Jordan, Terry Lovell, Richard Paterson, and John Stewart (London: British Film Institute, 1981), p. 48.

37. For a brief list of other cross-soap visits, see Beth Cochran, "For the Record: Soap Hopping," *Soap Opera Digest* 18, no. 16 (August 3, 1993): 85.

38. Another sign of the positive reception given to such transplants came in a *TV Guide* column dealing with unfounded rumors about various soap opera performers:

> **Rumor:** *General Hospital* refugee **Kin Shriner** is taking his Scotty Baldwin character to *Loving*. **Fact:** Get this: The terrifically talented Shriner wanted to join the show and was turned down flat—despite his massive following! *Ay caramba!* If *Loving* had as much sizzling drama on-air as it does backstage, it might not be sitting at the bottom of the Nielsens.

Michael Logan, "Soaps," *TV Guide* 42, no. 28 (July 9, 1994): 29.

39. More challenging than these prime-time visits, however, was the 1993 transplantation of two popular characters—attorney Eli (Alan Rosenberg) and legal secretary Denise (Debi Mazar)—from ABC's failed law drama *Civil Wars* to NBC's failing law drama *L.A. Law*, a move that, even more than the soap opera crossovers I've described, suggests a blurring of boundaries between different series, competing networks, and even, perhaps, between fictional characters and the actors who portray them.

40. Such an industry-produced mega-soap would, of course, be quite different from the fan-written crossover stories Henry Jenkins describes in *Textual Poachers*, pp. 170–71.

41. Andrew Goodwin attributes the idea of the "televisual supertext" to Nick Browne; cited in *Dancing in the Distraction Factory: Music Television and Popular Culture* (Minneapolis: University of Minnesota Press, 1992), p. 171. The connections with Raymond Williams's notion of "flow," developed in *Television: Technology and Cultural Form* (New York: Schocken Books, 1975), are obvious.

INDEX

Laura
Stempel
Mumford

has written
about TV,
women's fiction,
feminist theory,
style, and the
experience of being
an independent scholar.
She lives in Madison,
Wisconsin.